PUBLIC THEOLOGY
AND
POLITICAL ECONOMY

CHRISTIAN STEWARDSHIP IN MODERN SOCIETY

by
Max L. Stackhouse

WM. B. EERDMANS PUBLISHING CO. • GRAND RAPIDS
FOR
COMMISSION ON STEWARDSHIP
NATIONAL COUNCIL OF THE CHURCHES OF CHRIST
IN THE U.S.A.

DEDICATION

To ecumenical church leaders everywhere who,
as stewards of the Word, seek prophetic, priestly, and public ways
to guide our human stewardship of the world
toward a cosmopolitan commonwealth.

Copyright © 1987 Commission on Stewardship, National Council of Churches
Published by Wm. B. Eerdmans Publishing Co.
255 Jefferson Ave. S.E., Grand Rapids, MI 49503

Library of Congress Cataloging-in-Publication Data:

Stackhouse, Max L.
Public theology and political economy.

Includes bibliographical references.
1. Sociology, Christian. 2. Christianity and
politics. 3. Stewardship, Christian. I. Title.
BT738.S6955   1987   261.8   87-435

ISBN 0-8028-0267-2

Contents

Acknowledgments   vii

Introduction   viii

ONE: *By What Authority?*   1
        The "Quadrilateral" Touchstones of Authority   4
            Scripture   5
            Tradition   7
            Reason   10
            Experience   13

TWO: *Principles of a Public Theology*   17
        Creation and Liberation   18
        Vocation and Covenant   24
        Moral Law, Sin, and Freedom   27
        Ecclesiology and Trinity   30

THREE: *The Roots of Christian Sociology*   36
        The Fight Against Slavery   37
        The Rejection of "The Bloody Law of Tooth and Claw" 41
        The Affirmation of "Christ Transforming Culture"   43
        The Emerging Themes of "Social Christianity"   45

FOUR: *The Democratization of the Economic Order*   52
        Shailer Mathews and Christian Personalism   53
        Walter Rauschenbusch and Christian Prophecy   59
        Persons in Communities/Communities of Persons   64
        Spreading the Social Gospel   66
            The Sunday School Movement   66
            The Missions Movement   68
        Today: Christian Sociology in Decline   71

FIVE: *Ecumene and Economy*   75
Some Historical Ecumenical Statements   76
Some Historical Socioeconomic Theories   83
The Necessary Ethical Transformation of
  Weberian Theory   91

SIX: *Piety and Power*   94
The Multiple Facets of Political Power   96
Piety's Relationship to Politics: Some Limits   103

SEVEN: *Spirituality and the Corporation*   113
Possible Social Centers of Economic Organization   114
The Corporation: In Need of Theological Assessment   118
Defining the Corporation   122
The Religious Roots of the Corporation   125
Reforming the Spirituality of the Corporation   130

EIGHT: *Sacrament and Technology*   138
How Belief Affects the Development of Technology   141
The Bomb and the Computer: The Ambiguity of
  Technology Made Plain   147
Sacramental Symbols in a Technological Society   153

NINE: *Pluralism and the Future of Stewardship*   157
Pluralism: A Blessing and a Curse   158
The Necessary Pluralism of Society   163
The Professions: The New Complexities of Pluralism   167
The Future of Stewardship   174

Acknowledgments

While working on the questions addressed in this book for the Stewardship Commission of the National Council of Churches, I was invited to lecture at several other institutions, and I used these occasions to test and revise some of the materials in this volume. Indeed, some of the materials contained herein have been published in other forms on the basis of these other lectures. I wish to thank Union Theological Seminary, Richmond, Virginia, where I first presented some of the themes of Chapters One and Two (see an earlier article I wrote called "An Ecumenist's Plea for a Public Theology," in *This World* [Spring/Summer 1984], pp. 47-79). I also wish to thank Texas Christian University, where I was given the opportunity to speak at the annual Ministers' Week on themes found in Chapters Six, Seven, and Eight. I am also grateful to the scholarly society Biblical Theologians, to whom I first presented materials subsequently modified for publication by the Society of Biblical Literature and here presented in still another form in Chapters Three, Four, and Five (for the earlier version, see my essay entitled "Jesus and Economics," in *The Bible in American Law, Politics, and Political Rhetoric,* ed. James T. Johnson [Chico, Calif.: Scholars Press, 1985], pp. 107-51). And finally, parts of Chapter Nine were delivered as a lecture at a conference in India, where the problems of pluralism and interfaith dialogue are especially acute (see pp. 1-31 of vol. 29 of *Religion and Society,* published by the Christian Institute for the Study of Religion and Society, Bangalore, India). The whole was delivered in the 1986 Summer Session of the Vancouver School of Theology, to which I am also indebted. My thanks also to Kay Coughlin, Edith Gunn, and especially Mary Hietbrink of Eerdmans, who helped prepare this material for publication.

Introduction:
The Stewardship of
Word and World

I want to express my appreciation to the Commission on Stewardship of the National Council of the Churches of Christ for planting
the seed of this book by inviting me to give a series of lectures at
the annual "Winter Event" over the past three years. The topics the
commission discusses touch on some of the most important debates
presently before us in the ecumenical churches. Further, since the
early 1970s, when the commission first invited me to work with
them on these issues, I have been eager to extend and refine my
initial reflections on these matters.[1]

In the intervening years I have concentrated much of my research on cross-cultural and cross-historical perspectives on religious and social issues in projects that took me to Eastern Europe
and Asia several times. Exposure to these cultures and ideas has
forced me to modify some of my earlier views of political and economic life. Of special interest to me have been the ways in which
theological ideas interact with social forces and structures either to
support or to inhibit the development of human rights in civilization, and the ways in which ecumenical-theological concerns can
interact with a variety of contexts around the globe.[2]

1. See my article "Toward a Stewardship Ethic" in the *Andover Newton
Quarterly* 14 (1974): 245-66. The article is reprinted in *Teaching and Preaching
Stewardship*, ed. Nordan C. Murphy (New York: National Council of the Churches
of Christ in the U.S.A., 1985), pp. 87-111.

2. See my book *Creeds, Society, and Human Rights: A Study in Three
Cultures* (Grand Rapids: Eerdmans, 1984). See also *Apologia: Contextualization,
Globalization, and Mission in Theological Education*, forthcoming.

It has become increasingly clear to me that theological ideas play a quite decisive role in social life, a role frequently obscured by a number of contemporary modes of social analysis and by some ways of understanding the nature and character of theology. Indeed, the failure to recognize how important this role is tends of itself to induce a crisis both in religious organizations and in social analysis. Many people, including some clergy, doubt that religious ideas make much of an objective difference in the public domain, although they feel that these ideas should have such an impact. And many are uncertain about how to understand our contemporary social environment. Some features seem to manifest Christian values, while others seem directly to contradict these values. This confusion is particularly strong in the understanding of the political economy of modern life.

What I was asked to undertake in the "Winter Events" of 1983, 1984, and 1985 — under the title "The Word Becomes Flesh in a Consumeristic, Technologistic, and Pluralistic Society" — entailed a rather remarkable agenda, especially if we recognize that the term "Word" in this title is a translation from the New Testament *logos,* that *logos* is a term that has many levels of meaning, and that attempts to interpret the nature and character of modern society are as complex as the most subtle theological argument.

Yet the effort seemed worth it. Since the Enlightenment, many matters of religion, ethics, values, and meaning seem to have been relegated to the private, personal, and "subjective" spheres of life, quite removed from the public, social, and "objective" patterns of living. Indeed, some of the best social scientists writing today have noted that in this shift we may have lost something indispensable to the survival of civilization in the long run.[3]

In reflecting on these themes, I realized that a contemporary treatment of the Christian idea of stewardship must surely involve a double focus. It must involve both an interpretation of those reliable themes of theology that have import for public life and that in some measure can be given articulation in public discourse, and an interpretation of the political-economic structures of modern life. Indeed, the latter must be understood in terms of those moral and spiritual values (either creative or destructive) that guide it. Not everything in the theological tradition is equally relevant to a mod-

---

3. See Robert Bellah et al., *Habits of the Heart: Individualism and Commitment in American Life* (Berkeley and Los Angeles: University of California Press, 1985).

ern civilization, and not everything in modernity is subject to comment or approval by the theological tradition. A rather wide range of political and economic questions has always been technical and/or prudential in nature, and it is doubtful that Christian theology has, or should claim, any special competence to address such questions. Although many Christians may develop special skills in this area and many more may have very strong opinions, no one is about to be prevented from participation in the Christian communion for differing on matters of a technical or prudential sort, or for having opinions that differ from those of church leaders.

Of course, religions from time immemorial have influenced, and been influenced by, the political and economic worlds in which they have found themselves, but the demands on us in our contemporary environment may be quite distinctive. Today, many of those most engaged in dealing with economic and political matters, either as theorists or as practitioners, doubt whether it is proper to include anything "religious" in the way they understand "the real situation" or in the way they "do business." Personal piety is acceptable, but many seem to think it an intrusion for theologians to take up economic or political matters publicly. To be sure, fundamentalists on the right and liberationists on the left do so, but they are on the fringes of serious political and economic thought, even if one group makes liberals (the other conservatives) apoplectic. For most, faith is strictly personal, and questions of power and influence are entirely separate from it.

Theologically, however, it is hard to justify the view that God is one thing, mammon another, and that we can best serve them both by keeping them entirely separate. And sociologically, it is doubtful whether any civilization has kept them separate. There is something about all profound religious and social understandings of reality that is dissatisfied with such a dualism. To be sure, the divine is not the world, and distinctions have to be made. Yet any transcendent reality worth attending to has implications for what we think and do on earth. The eternal is relevant to history; the absolute is pertinent to the relative; the ideal modifies the material. On that all religions are agreed. Certainly Christian theology holds that when it speaks of the living God, it is speaking of something that reigns over all the world, whether all the world knows that or not. This God has, and must have, direct bearing on how we conduct worldly affairs. Thus, if we intend to deal with such "worldly" matters as power and wealth in a political economy, what we say cannot be merely another special-interest voice or another idiosyncratic expression of conviction entirely determined by social forces or economic interests. It must be something that makes sense as a norm or guide in wrestling with questions of public importance.

I will argue that a "public theology" is required. "Theology," properly understood, is not merely the rationalization of a private or particular faith. We have a special word for that: "confession." Theology involves critically examining the confession, determining whether it is worth having according to a defensible understanding of the *logos* of *theos* — that is, evaluating the confession according to its capacity to articulate a reliable and coherent knowledge of divine reality. To speak this way entails the conviction that it is possible to speak about the most important questions, such as God, in public discourse — in ways that can interact with other sciences and make sense among the people. It is called a "public" theology for two reasons. First, because that which we as Christians believe we have to offer the world for its salvation is not esoteric, privileged, irrational, or inaccessible. It is something that we believe to be both comprehensible and indispensable for all, something that we can reasonably discuss with Hindus and Buddhists, Jews and Muslims, Humanists and Marxists. Second, such a theology will give guidance to the structures and policies of public life. It is ethical in nature. The truth for which we argue must imply a viable element of justice, and its adequacy can be tested on that basis.

It is surely true that there are prerational and transrational elements in every religion, certainly in all ideas of God. But religion is not alone in that. It is difficult to interpret modern politics, economics, and technology without also recognizing the prerational and transrational elements in these areas of discourse and social life. Nor will I contend that one can logically argue to the truth of God. It may well be the case that the only logical view of reality derives from the conviction that a superordinate reality, being, or power that can be named "God" exists, even though many features of this "other" are beyond our comprehension. But my argument here is more limited. I attempt to show that it makes sense to undertake a joining of theology and social analysis in the quest for a grounded set of guidelines for public life in the modern world (see especially Chapters One and Two).

The current debates about our political economy (in theological circles especially) are polarized between the democratic capitalists and the democratic socialists. I have tried to be in conversation with both ends of this spectrum, and I have broken discussion only when the noun of each party became so central to the position taken that my partners in dialogue were willing to sacrifice the adjective. While no single political system is necessarily more "Christian" than others for all times, decisive biblical and theological principles press Christianity in a democratizing direction. I take democracy, with all its weaknesses, to be the best expression of basic theological principles in modern social life in this sense: any political or economic system that does not support the possibilities of pluralistic democratic governance under laws that protect basic human rights, minorities, and dissent is not theologically or ethically defensible in modern public discourse. Social democratization implies that the institutions shaping the common life ought to be structured for equitable opportunity, pluralistically ordered, and held accountable for the effects they have on people and on the human future. Also implied is the notion that a socialism that collectivizes everything into the hands of the state and a capitalism that leaves everything to the "possessive individualism" of privileged elites are simply not adequate descriptively or normatively.

I would be happier if the term "social democracy" were not already taken by certain political parties in Europe, because the term describes the way Christians might best think about political and economic issues. The noun is "democracy"; the adjective implies a regulating social conscience. Where democratic values and social concerns converge with economic viability, the political economy can be morally ordered or evaluated. The terms may be modern, but the basic idea is very old. It is implied in the formation of the early theological traditions when Christianity encountered Greco-Roman civilization, in major elements of the Reformation, and in the efforts during the last century to develop a "Christian sociology." A key purpose of this book is to reclaim and recast these traditions in view of contemporary conditions (see especially Chapters Three, Four, and Five).

The connecting term between a public theology and a social perspective on political economics is "stewardship." The first challenge of stewardship is the reasonable stewardship of theology, by which the various "words" of faith are assessed, refined, and — where appropriate — defended. The second challenge is to show that the key themes of theology can and do give normative guidance to political economy. Everyone who has studied these issues knows that the English word "stewardship" is a translation of the biblical Greek word *oikonomia*, which has been appropriated in the West in two ways. One definition moves in the direction of "the whole inhabited world," and thus refers to the structures of civilization that, under God, have brought a new interdependence to the globe. The other definition may be given as "the 'rule' or management of the household." From one meaning we have derived the modern understanding of "ecumenical" life in its broadest and deepest meanings, and from the other has come the modern discipline of economics as it has taken shape in the life of nations. This second meaning encompasses common decisions about managing the resources of the common life and developing the techniques and structuring the institutions to do so effectively. "Stewardship," at root, is about the relationship of Word to world, of ecumenical theology to political economics.

"Stewardship" is a particularly fortunate translation for what is here undertaken. It comes from Old English and reflects a practice of appointing particularly reliable workers to be wardens of the pig sty: *sty-wards*. These wardens, living under the "word" of the "lord" of the manor, were to become trustworthy custodians of those resources that were indispensable to the life and well-being of the whole community. They were to lovingly and prudently care for that over which they had authority.

When the ancient scriptures were being translated into English, it must have been an act of inspiration that brought the scholars to adopt and adapt this term. It does connect the several motifs decisive both for a compelling understanding of the gospel and for responsible living in community. All persons are to become stewards: servants of the ecumenical Lord. We are to become persons with an "office," having authority in the communal life. We are responsible for the physical resources necessary for existence, and we are expected to be diligent in the very earthy tasks assigned in the world, for the very fate of the community depends on our trustworthy custodianship.[4] Only in this context does the narrow definition of "stewardship" — voluntary contributions to the church — make sense. Indeed, we are prompted to give sacrificially only if spiritual obedience to the Lord's Word also effectively guides material existence in the world.

Embedded in the deeper and broader meanings of the term "stewardship" is the notion of an institutional arrangement. The decisive institution of public life was once the household. For good reasons, the older institutions have passed away, and new ones have taken their places. Thus, today "home economics" is not the center of the decisive questions as it once was. In modern complex

---

4. See Douglas John Hall, *The Steward* (New York: Friendship Press, 1984).

societies, the individual household, even that of some great ruler of a kingdom, is not the center of productivity, distribution, or even consumption, as it clearly was in the agricultural societies that reigned in most civilizations over most of human history. The factory, the industry, the transnational corporation, the global market, the bomb, the computer—all have drastically altered our political-economic situation. However, in much of their ecumenical witness, major religious groups have allowed themselves to offer only ad hoc reflections on how the "Word" that they hold to be true is related to these developments.

Christianity has influenced some of these changes, as we will see, but Christian treatments of stewardship have seldom tried to understand key features of modern institutional life—especially the modern corporation, aspects of modern technology, and the modern professions. Indeed, it is difficult to find serious institutional analysis in most of the modern literature on stewardship. Even such much-heralded statements on theology and economics as have recently issued from the Roman Catholic bishops of the United States and Canada, from the Presbyterian Church of the United States, and from the United Church of Christ contain relatively little on this front. To correct this imbalance, I will give significant attention to the institutional fabric of modern civilizations, in which and for which we are also to exercise stewardship (see especially Chapters Six through Nine).

As the reader will find, it is a primary contention of this effort that those who understand stewardship to mean nothing more than voluntary giving to the church are not so much wrong as too constricted in their vision. The implicit message of these chapters is this: when and if the churches reclaim, recast, teach, and enact the deeper and broader meanings of stewardship and offer interpretive and normative guidance to the complexities of modern political economy, those who catch the vision will be prompted to share, sacrificially, their resources.

At the end of each chapter is a series of themes, study aids, and questions for use in congregations or classes. These study materials have been prepared, at the request of the Stewardship Commission, by Ms. Paula Waters, a longtime lay theologian, Sunday School teacher, and stewardship advocate in the Twelfth Baptist Church, Roxbury, Massachusetts. Ms. Waters is currently also a vice president and business manager of Andover Newton Theological School as well as a financial consultant to a number of community organizations.

CHAPTER ONE

By What Authority?

In recent years the ecumenically oriented churches around the world have been speaking out vigorously on political and economic issues. That is as it should be, for we are confronted with discrepancies of wealth and poverty, abundance and hunger, and opportunity and dislocation that are scandals to conscience. Indeed, we do not have to look far to find such inequity. Who among the religiously and ethically sensitive does not feel anguish when confronted with homeless families, unemployed and aimless minority youth, and the disparities between those who enjoy plenty to the point of gluttony and those who form an apparently permanent underclass?

It is not clear that this anguish can be overcome by the predominant patterns of political and economic thought. The overwhelming tendency today is to hold that we can solve our problems with a combination of clarity about national interests, shrewdness about technology, and clever manipulations of government policies. That we need more practical insight into human interests, the uses of alternative technologies, and the probable effects of governmental policies is hardly debatable, but the problems may be deeper than that. The critical issues of stewardship are rooted in more profound moral and spiritual factors in life. Modern civilizations are unsure of what the moral rudders for life are, and they are in danger of substituting egocentric nationalisms, hedonistic consumerism, and private preference for those moral and spiritual principles that are much more deeply founded and that are necessary to the long-term viability of civilization.

The key problem is that today we do not have a profound public theology. That is, we do not have a deep and broad concept of what God requires of humanity in our public behaviors in a broken, divided, and threatened world. To be sure, we have all sorts of voices speaking out of petty little contexts and attempting to tell us that this or that "biblical politics" is the absolute revelation. And we have "civil religions" of a number of stripes all over the globe. Class and ethnic ideologies wearing the garb of religion also abound. Not infrequently, these become powerful and begin to affect national or international policies. But what we do not have is a reliable "science" by which we could assess the relative sense or nonsense of such postures. Indeed, we do not have a common language for speaking of theological matters in the public domain, of what the ultimate reality behind human life in community entails. The language of public moral and spiritual discourse is fractured. People place their technical or economic or political bets on what will bring advantage without paying conscious attention to the governing principles and purposes of life.

Of course, many of us maintain a deep personal piety. But when we face questions of polity and policy bearing on the public world, questions of structure and function in our political and economic life, we doubt whether these personal convictions do or should make any objective difference at all. Despite all the statements on social, political, and economic issues made by ecumenical churches, the new efforts by fundamentalists to exert political influence, and the surge of liberationism among the religious New Left, the *foundations* for moral and spiritual analysis are eroding, and the custodians of these foundations are not shoring them up. To put the matter another way (somewhat confrontationally), the ecumenically oriented churches have not always been good stewards of that which is their greatest treasure: a capacious theology, defensible in public discourse, that is able to link personal and social matters, ideal and material reality, memory and hope, private and public vision.

Some years ago Wallace Fisher pointed out that stewardship has most to do with being stewards of the Word, of theological truth; it is that above all which we are to nurture and cultivate, treasure and invest.[1] When that is clear, people will incarnate it in their lives and share resources generously. As I look at our present situation, I wonder whether our ecumenical churches have in fact

---

1. Fisher, *A New Climate for Stewardship* (Nashville: Abingdon, 1976).

invested their time, energy, and talents in the stewardship of the Word, that it might become embodied in our complex civilization, or whether we have been using up our theological capital without replenishing it. And I wonder if this is not particularly the case in the political and economic arenas of life.

Public theology is not absent in all areas of life. In 1979, the World Council of Churches sponsored the Conference on Faith, Science, and the Future, hosted by M.I.T.[2] This initiated a new dialogue between religion and the modern sciences that had been broken off since Galileo. This rift is not fully repaired, but such a conference indicates a new willingness on the part of theology to engage the contemporary material sciences in a fresh way — one promising for a public theology. And a few years ago the Roman Catholic bishops issued their pastoral letter on war and peace,[3] the first Roman Catholic document since the Reformation to be commended for congregational study by some twenty-seven Protestant denominations. This was also one of the great events of public theology in the recent memory of the church. It was equal in significance to the witness, a generation ago, of Martin Luther King, who brought priests and nuns into solidarity with free-church pastors, rabbis, and lay leaders of many faiths. He captured the moral imagination of the world on theological grounds to confront racism. Such events signal the profound stewardship of the modern ecumenical church on public issues. In these areas we must celebrate. But few comparable events have focused on the whole range of issues bearing on political economy.

In this first chapter, I want to ask a very preliminary question. When we begin to formulate a proposal about what the Word might be as it bears on political economics, how do we know whether the proposal is any good? What we seek, here at the outset, are the marks or warrants for an adequate public theology. What will guide the selection and definition of the "Word" of which we are stewards? Later we will ask about its content and its relationship to modern social history.

Some of the points that I am about to make will appear to be "abstract" at first, but this is not the problem that it might seem

---

2. See *Faith and Science in an Unjust World,* 2 vols., vol. 1: *Plenary Presentations,* ed. Roger Shinn; vol. 2: *Reports and Recommendations,* ed. Paul Abrecht (Geneva: WCC Press, 1980).

3. See *The Challenge of Peace: God's Promise and Our Response* (Ramsey, N.J.: Paulist Press, 1983).

to be. It is of course true that every claim that Christians make will be tested on the anvil of life. Every view must be capable of providing practical and direct guidance in facing particular questions as they arise. But it is also the case that we are never sure how practical things will come out in the long run. The data of history are never complete, and all dimensions of the questions we face daily are seldom clear. Thus we can never rely on practical matters alone. Indeed, we have to have some bases for assessing whether what seems practical is in accord with those higher principles of truth and justice that cannot be read from the facts of history alone. If we are to wrestle with these principles, we have no choice but to be abstract. The old adage is a good one: The most practical thing in the world is a good theory.

THE "QUADRILATERAL" TOUCHSTONES OF AUTHORITY

The warrants I suggest here are not my own. They are very ancient. They are, to be sure, given an especially crisp, modern articulation in the *The Book of Discipline* of the United Methodist Church, although they are by no means confined to that confessional communion, and there is little evidence that the Methodists are better at utilizing these principles than many others. What the Methodists have done is to bring into rather cogent formulation the key classical ecumenical criteria by which we can assess the various proposals for theological meaning as they rise and fall in human history. These principles are Scripture, Tradition, Reason, and Experience — the so-called "quadrilateral."

Over the centuries, various confessional families have seized these touchstones of authority in varying ways. Roman Catholics (in comparison with others) have been especially dependent on Tradition and Reason as formulated by a magisterium; Protestants have relied heavily on Scripture and Experience as interpreted by great reformers. Fundamentalists tend to argue on the grounds of Scripture alone, and liberationists tend to celebrate Experience as the center of everything. Philosophers tend to stress Reason alone (and sometimes include Experience in it), while Eastern Orthodox believers invoke Tradition above all. The quadrilateral suggests that we need all four touchstones, each constantly refining and elaborating our understanding of the others. Of course, this implies that we Protestants, if we want to be genuinely ecumenical, need to pay more attention to Tradition and Reason than we usually do, and that the task of constructing and reconstructing public theology is never done.

Public theology turns to this quadrilateral in a way that the more confessional accents in the several traditions of the West may not have had in mind. If these criteria are to be pertinent to modern political economy, we have to see them in a new global perspective. They serve, so to speak, as four boundaries of the playing field of public theological discussion. They are not God, the final authority, but they point to God's limits. They offer guidelines that show us when we are most likely to be speaking about God, and when we are out of bounds and worshiping the artifacts of our own imaginations. They do not prescribe how each person or each community of faith must play the game. Different persons and different communities will play out their religious, philosophical, and social styles differently, with various kinds of coaching in differing circumstances. What these touchstones of authority do, however, is tell us whether the particular orientations we have are in the ballpark, whether we are engaged in the same game. With this image in mind, let us survey these four criteria as they might apply to a public theology.

Scripture

The Holy Bible is universally accepted as a source and norm of faith in Christianity. Its influence on Western culture generally is vast, and it is increasingly influential in Africa and Asia — both directly, through the remarkable expansion of the church in the nineteenth and twentieth centuries, and indirectly, through the influence it has had on Western culture. As many other cultures modernize by adopting "Western" modes of thought as quickly as possible (even while protesting them at every turn), scriptural motifs become contextualized in cultures from which they were not derived.

Other religious traditions also have clearly defined sacred scriptures — most notably the Pali Canon of Theravada Buddhism and the Koran of Islam. Wherever a sacred scripture is accepted as normative in any sense, people indicate by accepting it that they believe the forebears who formed the canon made essentially correct decisions. The implication is that the forebears rightly discerned — and believers today should concur — that in and behind the multitude of sometimes disjointed, certainly pluralistic witnesses that are contained in scriptures, often written under all sorts of historical conditions and at the hands of a variety of authors and redactors now lost in legend, the inspiration of that which is truly holy may be found.

Many have noted that the devil can prove anything by Scripture, and we cannot avoid the fact that scriptures have to be interpreted. One cannot simply open this or that holy book at will and read directly the thoughts of God. The process of discerning any scripture's meanings is considerably more complex. In part, we must rely on the other principles of the quadrilateral. We have to rely on Tradition — that is, on what the company of the faithful have found in the text over the centuries and how they have utilized these meanings in multiple contexts. And we have to rely on Experience — specifically on that experience of inspiration by which we become participants in that Spirit which stands behind the words. Both of these may provide secure knowledge of what Scripture is about, but these remain "private" in the sense of being "privileged" to a particular tradition. For a public theology, we must also attend to what the historians, archaeologists, linguistic experts, and scholarly commentators tell us. And in large measure they rely on Reason and demonstrate that later scripture interprets earlier scripture, and that reinterpretation has been accepted as normative. How does this work?

Perhaps I can schematically present the point by reference to the Christian Scripture:

$$\frac{\text{Moses said}}{\text{his time}} \cong \frac{\text{The Psalmist sang}}{\text{his context}} \cong \frac{\text{The Prophets spoke}}{\text{their days}} \cong$$

$$\frac{\text{The Apostles wrote}}{\text{in their situation}} \cong \frac{\text{(Tradition has said)}}{\substack{\text{(over centuries} \\ \text{in many contexts)}}} \cong \frac{\text{What shall we say?}}{\substack{\text{How do we understand} \\ \text{our world?}}}$$

Each interpreted the previous writers and felt in continuity with them, although each also felt compelled to say something different. The key question, of course, is this: What are we to say in our time? How do we understand the Scriptural "Word" for today when we know that it has been given multiple articulations with different accents, both because it is spoken to or in specific contexts and because it has been refined, revised, or elaborated over time? The answer is that we have to discover and articulate, perhaps in new ways, scriptural themes that are simultaneously congruent with ($\cong$) the development of normative scriptures, pertinent to our context, and open to further refinement or elaboration in the future, just as the Word of Scripture has been. If we wish to test our sense of what is true according to Scripture, we cannot simply repeat what one or another passage says and settle the matter. Nor can we simply pick out things that we like and leave the rest alone. Surely we must engage in a rather subtle analysis to see (1) which of the things these authors said are only and specifically for the particular context in which they are speaking, (2) which of the things are eternally true and just — constant and valid for all times and places, (3) which things reflect development toward a fuller and richer view that we have to extend further in order to be faithful to what these authors originated, and (4) which things function in our contexts in such a way that they point toward the relief of malaise, toward the hope of reconciliation, forgiveness, and peace with justice, as those messages did in earlier times (and in the development of Tradition) — even if we say things that in some ways seem to be at odds with earlier messages because the times and contexts are so different. In all of these we have to have a message that will make public sense. If it does not, we tend to discredit not only our message but the scriptures on which we rely. The use of Scripture as a boundary line in a public theology, then, is both a way of testing our contemporary claims about what is adequate as a "word" for today, and a way of testing the adequacy of Scripture and its interpretation to provide civilization with the spiritual and moral principles of meaning able to guide life. Public theology, in other words, uses Scripture in an inevitably apologetic way. It has to make the case ever anew that an appeal to Scripture is able both to be congruent with the ancient writings and to provide the foundations for public discourse and action in the face of contemporary realities.

Tradition

Tradition, as a touchstone of authority, is similar. Facets of the Renaissance and the Reformation (and more of the Enlightenment) saw Tradition as simply the accumulation of man-made conventions designed to displace the authority of Scripture (or the clear wisdom of Reason) for the benefit of the few. Tradition was blamed for distorting experience, inhibiting science, and holding human minds in bondage to pompous priestcrafts. Many Protestants and some Catholics and Jews have adopted this view and have tried to hold in "pristine purity" only that which the Prophets or Jesus taught. They believe that "Tradition" has obscured the "Word" by mixing the "pure" biblical message with the philosophical, socio-political, legal, and ecclesiastical constructions of humans. The consequence has been a particular kind of modern parricide: only by destroying the witness of our forebears and returning to the original message fixed in the past do we think we make "progress" by "return."

When Tradition is accepted as a criterion of validity in a public theology, the case for the contributions of forebears has to be made anew in each generation. The effort always injects a note of conservatism into the discussion, although demanding that Tradition be interpreted through the prisms of Scripture, Reason, and Experience prevents such conservatism from becoming reactionary and simply glorifying some golden age. In considering Tradition, we have to ask this question: Had we been there (in critical moments of past decision that have shaped our history) and had at our disposal the knowledge, options, and sensibilities of the age in which previous decisions were made, with whom would and should we have sided? The question forces caution in our assurance that the more contemporary a perspective, the more wonderful it is. It deprovincializes our sense of "now," as if all things important are new. If we honor Tradition, we develop a certain respect for the possible wisdom of those who struggled with issues that anticipated those now before us. We acknowledge the possibility that the great ecumenical decisions of the past might have been valid in certain major respects. The more we attend to Tradition, the more we are inclined to pray that we do half so well in our own contexts.

No one can live without roots. To have one's tradition destroyed is to be a victim of cultural, social, or religious genocide. Today we apply this principle to many small cultures in danger of being swallowed by modernity, but we frequently fail to apply it to those civilizational roots of modern complex, industrial, democratic societies that are much larger and more determinative for humanity than those of the tiny, scattered tribes discovered by anthropologists. Such neglect brings not genocide but suicide. The future will extend only so far as our critical memories of cultural, social, and religious roots allow. The question is, Which roots are the deepest, the broadest, and the most nourishing?

Whoever repeats the creeds of the churches; whoever has a sense of what is a "proper" way to conduct a worship service, a sacrament, a rite, or a ritual; whoever identifies himself or herself as a "liberal," "conservative," "radical," or "orthodox" believer;

whoever understands his or her religious identity as a Protestant, Catholic, Shivite Hindu, Zen Buddhist, or Sufi Muslim — this individual has already given a provisional answer to the question of roots. Even those who cannot give such a specific answer often show that they are in traditions by their patterns of thought and action and by their senses of obligation and responsibility. To fail to take Tradition as a conscious criterion by examining it, testing it, and using it selectively as a test for contemporary life is to be shaped by traditions unwittingly. Indeed, lack of conscious awareness plunges us into life contradictions that impoverish our theological sensitivity and our public discourse. If our religious orientations are antitechnological but our life decisions depend on increased technology, if we live in and by incorporated institutions but hold corporate economies to be evil, if we utilize the pluralism of constitutional democracy to advocate totalitarian or anarchic religions, we become self-estranged victims of unacknowledged pasts. Or we drift in the immediacies of the day, all sails with no rudder.

For the most part, Tradition can be seen as the attempt of faith to respond to complex problems not answered explicitly by the events that originally induced the faith and generated the Scriptures. In the West, this had to do first with the encounter of the Hebraic perspectives and the message of Jesus with the complexities of Greco-Roman and feudal civilizations, and subsequently with the industrializing environments of Northern Europe and America; presently it has to do with the rapidly changing cultures of "postindustrial society," the emergence of "lesser-developed nations" from eras of stagnation or dependency, and the recent transformation toward a "universal civilization." It is in Tradition that we find not only patterns of worship but also multiple efforts to spell out the criteria (1) for distinguishing between justifiable and unjustifiable uses of coercive power in society, (2) for living with moral integrity in economically and technologically complex civilizations, (3) for the structuring of authority for responsible leadership in multiple contexts, and (4) for developing the basic principles of human rights and of viable economic systems. None of these criteria is immediately clear from any of the great scriptures, and to wrestle with these traditions is to recognize the ongoing unveiling of God's purposes in the Tradition that stretches from biblical days to the modern world. The movement toward these public theological principles involved numerous travesties. Most of the destructive heresies are still living options; some things that were called heresies turned out to be constructive theological insights. It is only by the knowledge of Tradition that we can see how mistakes were made and how they were sometimes corrected. Tradition as the dynamic story of the connection between Scripture and successive encounters with civilizational complexities is indispensable to our understanding of both past and present. To ignore its wisdom (as an ahistorical generation is inclined to do) is to disarm our minds and our common life.

In brief, it seems that we should make a presumption in favor of the basic and ecumenically accepted principles of Tradition as a second boundary for public theology. We may well have to reconsider and revise this boundary if our beliefs about the past prove, upon investigation, to be historically unsupported, or they are clearly not able to connect with Scripture, Reason, and Experience. Further, the global encounter with other traditions will bring new patterns to the ongoing process of tradition formation. But we should not decide beforehand that Tradition is nonsense, although that decision conveniently excuses us from serious engagement with anything but our present selves. The "cronocentrism" of our times presumes an infallibility for our own age and contemporary insight that the evidence does not warrant.

Reason

The third point of the quadrilateral is Reason. At various moments in history, rationalist or utilitarian forms of Reason attempted, with some success, to undercut the claims of Scripture and Tradition. Today, many who do not accept either the Bible or ecumenical Tradition are also skeptical of Reason. Reason seems so cold, so calculating, so technical, so pretentiously objective and elitist. How can this be a touchstone of anything really important like God, human identity, and the delicate tissues of human society? Is it also the responsibility of theology to be a steward of Reason? Many theological students, pastors, and other religious leaders do not like logic, philosophical argument, or tests of coherence and consistency. Indeed, they relativize Reason by suggesting that the logic of females, or of Asia or Africa, or of another age is entirely different from our Western, masculine, modern logic that has led the world to the brink of nuclear crisis and ecological destruction. Some believe this so deeply that they simply block out any evidence to the contrary — including the rather well-documented fact that women of all cultures, Buddhists, Hindus, Muslims, and tribal philosophers both ancient and modern all use syllogisms, the rules of the excluded middle, induction, deduction, analysis, dialectic, synthesis, and presumptions of cause and effect. These skeptics also overlook the fact that the denial of the universality of Reason was one of the most important philosophical groundings of Fascism. Others, more constructively, offer critiques of the ways in which white Western males have employed Reason in lopsided fashion, critiques that identify its parochial elements and point toward universal and inclusive patterns of human rationality.

Some of this protest is justified. Some varieties of human rationality do falsify the human condition. Some speak only of rationalized means without any reference to ends or first principles and thus deny that one can speak reasonably about why we should rationalize means in the first place. But this is never what theology has meant by the concept of Reason. It has always been suspicious of those forms of Reason ever in the employ of concupiscent ends, and of those human rationalizations whereby ingenious arguments can be constructed to deceive the conscience and justify the grossest prejudice. Nevertheless, theology has honored Reason as a gift of grace whereby the "image of God" in humans is able to know, by "right reason," something of the reality of God.

What is important about this for our present purposes is that the claims of faith and of conviction have to make sense across numerous boundaries — confessional, cultural, sexual, racial, linguistic, ideological, and even left-brain and right-brain hemispheric boundaries. In short, "right" reason is that which makes human communication possible. We have to be able to speak of theological matters in ways that are coherent, consistent, and compelling to the cosmopolitan dimensions of the human mind, or we will not be heeded. Reason may not convert the heart, but nonsense is out of bounds. God does not require that we lie, distort logic, believe what we know cannot be so, or impose private logics in universal and public contexts. The modern suspicion by "secular humanists" of much that passes for theology is properly based on this recognition.

Early in Christian history an intriguing question was posed: Could faithful believers meet Plato and Aristotle in heaven? The question asks if, in the infinite economy of God, those who could not have known the gospel but are duly honored for their Reason can have an honored place in the Kingdom. The answer is that because they exercised Reason — a gift of God to all humans — with such diligent care, God will save them as witnesses to pious fools.

All sane people use Reason in religion. When someone of whatever faith claims to have a religious insight, we test it by

Reason. If the insight is so ineffable that it cannot be communicated, public theology need not take it seriously. If it does not make any sense at all after we try to get inside the logic of the insight, we dismiss it. If a mode of reasoning is bound to esoteric experiences or to particular cultural, ethnic, or gender groupings so that anyone outside them cannot know what they mean, it may well continue to function in private arenas, but it is of no significance to public theology. Further, when something is understandable but only within such a confined frame of reference that it cannot be generalized without destroying serious public discourse, we need not take it as a possible position to which we should convert. I would argue that this is the case with the rhetoric of the Ayatollah Khomeini, with aspects of the sermons of Jerry Falwell, with dimensions of the brilliant, angry fulminations of Mary Daly, with most of the sayings of Sai Baba, and with all of what I understand of James Jones. But of course I would have to make my case in each instance by Reason, and I would have no right to expect that anyone should believe anything in my argument if it does not meet the test of Reason.

One must be careful in speaking of Reason in theological matters because there are aspects of faith and belief that are transrational or prerational. The heart may well have reasons that the mind knows not of. Further, it is surely the case, as Ronald Green has argued, that people have to choose to be reasonable, and many refuse to make that choice.[4] Certainly there have been moments in the history of serious religious thought when pietism and fideism so dominated discussions of Christian thought that it was difficult to tell whether what was being said was subrational or transrational. The only clue was found in the participants' efforts to offer elaborate reasons about why their rationally ambiguous positions should be heeded. Theology in its several dimensions — only some of which are of moment to a public theology — does deal with matters of religious mystery, passion, and angst that are beyond the capacity of Reason to induce or exhaust. But in naming these by the use of multidimensional symbols, theology makes these matters

---

4. Green, *Religious Reason: The Rational and Moral Basis of Religious Belief* (New York: Oxford University Press, 1978); Cf. also Nicholas Wolterstorff, *Reason within the Bounds of Religion* (Grand Rapids: Eerdmans, 1984); John H. Whittaker, *Matters of Faith and Matters of Principle: Religious Truth Claims and Their Logic* (San Antonio, Tex.: Trinity University Press, 1981); and *Faith and Rationality: Reason and Belief in God,* ed. Alvin Plantinga and Nicholas Wolterstorff (Notre Dame: University of Notre Dame Press, 1983).

accessible to critical examination and reasonable discourse. Such moments at their deepest are not irrational; they are what Paul Tillich once called "reason in ecstasy."

A final observation about Reason is that in a society where ignorance of Scripture and Tradition is common, and in a world where various scriptures and traditions must encounter one another, Reason is an indispensable criterion of public discourse about the most important questions. A public theology will be open to "free thinking," doubt, and critical thought. It will draw on and include insights from nontheological sciences. Indeed, if we want people to attend to Scripture and Tradition, we have to give convincing reasons why they should do so in ways that they can comprehend. We have to show that heeding these principles makes psychological, economic, political, and social sense as well as metaphysical and moral sense.

Reason operates with and on materials that it does not, by itself, fully supply. A good bit of Reason is formal, the sort of thing *logic* deals with. The material with which it works in theology and ethics is partially supplied by Scripture and Tradition, by which it is already partially organized. It is also partially given by Experience, the fourth and last principle of the quadrilateral.

Experience

Experience has particularly to do with emotion and feeling and with that kind of knowledge that is directly built up through doing something. But not all experience is equally important. It is difficult to argue that the experience of oppression, injustice, and hate reveals that which we may take as a touchstone of authority. Indeed, it is the experience of creativity, construction, and the overcoming of destruction and decay that is important. For example, a carpenter knows by experience how to measure and cut the first time without error, and a violinist knows by experience how to make notes on a page sing.

Any viable public theology will have to touch the resonances of what people already know by "experience." It must encounter the wisdom already present in the sensibilities and practice of life. To be sure, people know many things derived from their feelings and habits. But not all are of lasting or public import, and one of the most remarkable facts of modern life is that experiences differ so much that it is not they which bind humans together. That is the inevitable weakness of empirical theology: it does not provide the criteria by which we can judge between the valid and the trivial experience. Yet empirical theologies know that any serious public theology cannot violate the deepest emotional fabric of human existence nor the profound mores by which people make daily life bearable, for theology presumes that God is present in the deepest experience of life. What it can do is assist in the identification and selection of those dimensions of feelings and mores that are of common import. Public theology, in other words, respects the delicate tissues of sentiment, civility, virtue, and awareness by which nonintellectuals all of the time — and intellectuals most of the time — hold the fragments of their lives together.

There is peril in this. Many people simply want religion to make them feel good, to approve what they already do and think. And there are enough clergy (and psychologists, self-help "experts," advertisers, and political propagandists) who will pander to this desire with cheerful ingratiation. But justifiable scorn for them does not negate the fact that the lessons of Experience need to be treated with tenderness, even if they require criteria from beyond the experience itself to evaluate the experience.

The truth and justice that a public theology attempts to articulate is rooted in a God of compassion, and that truth as it is told, as well as we can tell it, must be spoken in love. Loving regard for human experience is the fourth criterion, the completing boundary for a public theology. I think it can be shown that what people want more than anything else in experience is love. Love is the experiential knowledge of God's truth and justice. We all want love because we know, at some level of our consciousness, that love is what makes experience meaningful. If public modes of discourse do not convey this love and guide it as the core of human experience, all the substitutes for love become the sources of "inspiration" and motivation — sensuality, avarice, clubbiness, clannishness, hyperpatriotism in the guise of love of country on the right, and the impassioned embrace of the vindictive resentment of the dispossessed against everybody else on the left.

Most of those who provide leadership and guidance for civilization do not take love and compassion as critical principles of their policies or their interpretation of the dynamics of political economy. Seldom do they focus on those patterns of belief or affection that bond individuals to one another and to communities. Can we say that politicians and bureaucrats or political science have love as a criterion for their arts and sciences? Business and labor or economics? Lawyers and criminologists or jurisprudence?

Academics and administration or pedagogy? Science and mechanics or technology? People in these fields may be loving, but the connections between their personal dispositions, their professional skills, and the public policies they advocate remain obscure. "Experience" often becomes little more than "empiricism" as an ideology of objectivity. However much we may learn from these disciplines about some facts of the world, we must never allow them to rule the human understanding of Experience. Public theology takes compassion as a public and not merely a private principle, one compatible with Scripture, Tradition, and Reason. Indeed, it claims that only this principle can complete the boundaries of public discourse in such a way as to cure the malaise of modern society, provide a fuller framework for ecumenical perspectives, and induce relative assurance about whether proposals for governing themes in public discourse are on the playing field of viability. Thus public theology will not alienate itself from the people, the cultures, and the societies it hopes to influence and guide. Even its prophetic denunciations will be spoken in and with compassion. It will engage human experience lovingly.

If, then, Scripture, Tradition, Reason, and Experience serve as the warrants for speaking theologically with authority, what is their content? This is the question we take up in Chapter Two.

Study Questions

This chapter argues that Christian stewardship begins in the public stewardship of the Word, and that the four most important touchstones, or bases, for any "public theology" are Scripture, Tradition, Reason, and Experience.

1. Should Christians be involved in developing a public theology? Does a public theology differ from private belief? From a "confession" or an "affirmation" by a faith community?

2. How ought we to respond to the belief held by some that religion should not be involved in social, political, or economic matters?

3. In a pluralistic world with many religions, faiths, and philosophies, on what basis can the Christian church be heard as authoritative? Does a Christian public theology mean that Christians are absolutely correct and everyone else is wrong?

4. What commonalities exist between Christianity and other religions, philosophies, or social theories? What differences exist between them?

5. If Scripture, Tradition, Reason, and Experience become the bases of authority for faith and practice in a civilization, does a public theology based on them change over time?

6. What are some current examples of the dangers of emphasizing one base of authority over others — Scripture, for example. Can we properly understand Scripture without relying on Tradition, Reason, and Experience?

7. What are some examples of how the interpretation of Scripture has been influenced by Tradition, and how the worship, witness, and work of the church has been altered as a result? Has Tradition contributed to the understanding of theology and public ethics? Has it detracted from that understanding? How has society been affected by the development of Tradition?

8. If Reason is used as a base for public theology, what are the criteria of reasonability? Do you think of "reason" in terms of logic, science, or philosophy? Do you think of "reason" as practical effectiveness? How do you know when something is unreasonable? Are Scripture, Tradition, and Experience beyond, against, or incompatible with Reason?

9. Should public theology be guided by Experience? What kind of experience? What different types of emotions and encounters play a part in how decisions are made on social, economic, and political matters? Are all experiences equally valid in religion and society?

10. What should be the responsibility of the individual and of the local church in the development of a public theology? What difference would such a theology make at local, national, and international levels?

11. If Christians today undertook "stewardship of the Word" in the context of society, what impact do you think it might have
   a) on environmental issues?
   b) on questions of social justice?
   c) on debates about war and peace?
   d) on science?
   e) on politics?
   f) on matters of racism, sexism, and cultural bias?
   g) on economics?
   h) on the financial support of religious institutions?

CHAPTER TWO

Principles of a Public Theology

We have attempted to identify the touchstones of authority for a public theology, and we have recognized that we must appropriately recast our ways of speaking about them for our ecumenical, global, interreligious, and pluralistic age. Scripture, Tradition, Reason, and Experience, in constant interaction, remain the guides for the reconstruction of a public theology. They demand of each generation the fresh articulation of what these imply for the problems of the age. As we face the particular problems of the stewardship of our contemporary political economy, we will have to ask what themes from these resources are capable of providing us with normative guidance.

The attempt to identify key perennial themes and to relate them to contemporary conditions implies that humans can know something reliable about "godly" matters, that these are pertinent to and can be argued in the public domain, and that a primary responsibility of the church is to preach, teach, and actualize these ultimate principles of meaning and life in social life. If the church's witness is not based on these, we have nothing to say in the world that cannot be better handled in the interest group, the caucus, the party, the boardroom, the union hall, the advocacy group, or the bureaucracy.

Ten decisive themes seem appropriate to the content of a public theology. These themes may not be exhaustive, but they do exemplify the kinds of motifs indispensable to overcoming the theological malaise of modernity. Each of these themes provides a coherent and compelling answer to a perennially vexing human question. Each answer also contains claims about what is ultimately true and just, as these bear implications directly pertinent to the stewardship of modern political economies. Today, different branches of the Christian community are focused on one or another of these themes, and each group sometimes becomes so fixed on one theme that the larger picture is lost. Indeed, in some cases the singular concentration becomes so constrictive that any who do not follow the theological fragment that the group takes as the whole are informally excommunicated. This will become clear as we identify one theme taken from the chief insight of the fundamentalists and a second taken from the modern liberationists. These two populist religious movements, which make older tensions between "conservatives" and "liberals" look like minor intramural quibbles, are among the fastest-growing movements in religion today. Both are narrow and constrictive in method and substance. But we must attempt to grasp what measure of truth and justice they contain and what it is about them that so many find compelling. Then we can set their insights into a larger frame. The remaining themes we will examine come from the shared "classical" motifs of theology. I have selected them because I believe they illustrate key elements for a coherent theological vision for the renewal of public life in complex modern civilizations.

CREATION AND LIBERATION

The first theme is *creation.* Christians, Jews, Muslims, most Hindus, and many followers of tribal religions believe in a Creator God on whom the world depends. But this view has been challenged by modern science since the time of Darwin. In response, the rise of Christian fundamentalism has been one of the more remarkable developments of twentieth-century religion. Fundamentalists have frequently argued for creationism, the view that God created the world and all forms of life at a given moment of time.

Fundamentalism is a distinctly modern phenomenon in Christianity. It entails a series of views about Scripture that have been viewed as heretical for most of theological history. In the twentieth century, however, when many have decided that the idea of heresy is outmoded and that all religious views are equal because all are equally irrelevant and idiosyncratic, Christian fundamentalism has developed with increasing force. Its primary target has been the

Darwinian views of evolution (biological, cosmological, and social). What gives this movement power and energy, I submit, is that its adherents know something important and true, although they have not yet articulated their perspective in a coherent way. Still, they are struggling more energetically than ecumenical thinkers today with the decisive question, "Why is there something and not merely nothing?"

The fundamentalists who hold to creationism are wrong, of course, about the scientific evidence. That we need not debate. They are also wrong in their insistence that we must force the data into patterns that accord with their particular interpretations of Scripture. And they are wrong in trying to get laws passed that will allow the propagation of sectarian views in the public schools. However, they have recognized something theologically that is of fundamental import beyond the issue of how science is taught in public schools. And until their valid insight on the other side of their error is recognized, the issues they raise are likely to distort public discussion.

What is valid behind their anxious and constrictive militance is their assertion that intellectual, educational, and scientific integrity is threatened today by certain widespread presuppositions. These presuppositions include the following: (1) that the world is an accident; (2) that life is a chance pattern that has a logic, if there is one at all, of mutations by material causes alone; (3) that humanity has no "quality of dignity" other than beasts do (except possibly a somewhat larger brain); (4) that the natural processes of change are disconnected from any divine purposes or principle; and (5) that religious belief is an outmoded, mythological way of trying to know how the world works, a way now displaced by science. The creationists disagree with the post-Darwinian reductionists, who presume (and demand the presumption from others) that there is neither a divine order, design, or intention governing the universe nor any higher law for guiding life than that which can be found in the survival of particular gene pools by successful adaptation to changing material environments. Religion, culture, patterns of civilization, and questions of truth or justice are understood to be the adaptive constructs of species or subspecies groupings attempting to gain dominance over resources, territory, or reproductive capacity, while nature and its dynamic laws, empirically observed, are seen to be the only point of reference by which to judge what is true.

The creationists know that this perspective is not adequate.[1] They are able to see, with more justification than their arguments supply, that this view denies the possibility of a God behind and beyond nature who is more important than nature itself, and that "nature" is to be seen as "creation" — a secondary and not the primary source and norm of reality, truth, and righteousness. If life "naturally" is bloody in tooth and claw, and if the future seems "naturally" to belong only to the "successful" fighters, adapters, and breeders, the creationists know that there is another, more ultimate reference point by which we ought to order our fighting, adaptation, and breeding. The creationists know the reference point by which we can discipline our instincts, tame our passions, assess our civilization, guide our patterns of interaction, and structure our lives together. All human science ought to be conducted in the service of a truth and righteousness greater than the constructions of the strong or the smart at any given moment of developmental flux. Indeed, science, at its deepest levels, must meet the tests of moral and spiritual values as well as those that accord with factual description. The ultimate mysteries of biology, of the cosmos, and of sociocultural development, the creationists implicitly claim, have a metaphysical-moral basis that cannot be ignored without doing damage to scientific truth.

It is perhaps easy to see why creationists also argue for prayer in the public schools and for the protection of the right to form independent schools where such invocation is not permitted. They hold that learning, teaching, and science are best conducted in an arena where one thinks and studies with a bowed head before that reality that is greater than the object of immediate investigation. Nature is to be treated in the context of reverence toward that which brought it into existence, and the natural patterns of life — internal to our psyches and external in the world — may have to be reordered according to a higher standard of truth and justice if these natural patterns lead to hellish consequences. Students not exposed to the great creation myths of world religions and not forced to confront the question of why the universe exists and why life should be seen as a gift (even where it is mean, harsh, and short) are educationally deprived. A generation that cannot understand the symbols of the Book of Genesis as truth claims (about the goodness of creation and the implications of the Fall) will find

---

1. See George Marsden, *Fundamentalism and American Culture* (New York: Oxford University Press, 1980).

the greatest art, literature, and poetry of civilization incomprehensible and will encourage an illiterate scientism.

The potential implications of this fundamentalist position for ecological constraint and the ethical uses of technology are extensive even if they are only crudely articulated by the advocates of creationism (in part because the fundamentalists lack a sacramental tradition that would be consistent with and give stability to their deepest insight). However, without a public theology that places the results of modern biological, cosmological, and social sciences in the most comprehensive context of the mystery of God's creativity, we lack the intellectual, spiritual, and moral resources to deal with the explosion of arrogant exploitations of the earth. In this case, science is likely to become less and less a quest for truth and more and more a handmaiden of techniques for manipulation, available on demand to the highest bidder and subject only to the constraints of human imagination.

The same logic is behind the creationists' resistance to abortion on demand. In sexuality and procreation, humans participate in the mystery of God's creativity with an awe apparently not present in animals. The formation of new life for humans is not only a biophysical event but also *a spiritual and moral event* that may well entail responsibilities we might wish to avoid but ought not to avoid. Again, our capacity to adjust the world to our wishes through technology needs to be constrained by a wider and deeper kind of understanding that puts science and technology in a more ultimate context.

At the other contemporary extreme we find *liberationism.* This second new phenomenon of modern religious life focuses on history and its patterns. The governing question of liberationism is, Can humans find fulfillment by social change? Liberationists answer this question with a clear "yes," an answer based on the belief that oppressed peoples are inspired by the Spirit of God to resist the principalities and powers of domination, overthrow the pharaohs of the world, and discover new possibilities of autonomy, freedom, community, and human fulfillment. Change — indeed, revolutionary change in history — is the inexorable movement toward the fulfillment of God's divine purpose for humanity.

Liberationism is based on a profound and valid insight that gives it its compelling quality. Liberationists know that the only God worth worshiping is biased in favor of the oppressed, and that truly pious living involves active social engagement for and advocacy of their rights. Liberationists know that much of science, philosophy, and religion is an ideological construction designed to protect the interests of the powerful against the weak. They also know of a godly justice that "has scattered the proud in the imagination of their hearts, . . . put down the mighty from their thrones, . . . exalted those of low degree; . . . [and] filled the hungry with good things" (Luke 1:51-53). They recognize that a compassionate righteousness must be characteristic of every morally and spiritually viable movement in human history. They see that every ideology, regime, program, or plan that pretends to provide salvation for human life is false if it does not challenge the pretense of the arrogant and open horizons of hope to those who suffer. As liberationists rehearse their liturgies of sins — racism, classism, sexism, imperialism, and colonialism — they correctly identify the perils of complex civilizations that arbitrarily arrogate privileges to some and condemn others to positions of fixed inferiority.

Frequently, however, these real discernments of evil are wed to a single philosophy of history that is indistinguishable from Marxist dialectics, and that necessitates the consolidation of political, economic, and social power in the hands of a single revolutionary party in the name of "the people." Those who share the liberationists' diagnosis of wrong but who offer alternative prescriptions or doubt that radical social change alone can bring human fulfillment are excommunicated, marginalized, silenced, or exiled.

The liberationists have seldom made the case for their position much better than the fundamentalists have made the case for their stance. That is why liberationism is often treated as "ideology" rather than theology. Frequently liberationists simply affirm their perspective on historical movement and social change toward "the Kingdom" as dogmatically as the fundamentalists speak of "creation," and they draw their social science from models as outmoded as those scientific models used by the creationists. With reference to both we are tempted to pray, "Lord, save us from these righteous ones." Liberationists selectively use Scripture in a proof-texting way while criticizing fundamentalists for doing just that. For instance, when they select the Exodus as the paradigm of the Bible to govern interpretation, they ignore the biblical witness about the economic failures in Israel that drove the children into Pharaoh's hands, and they overlook the fact that after the Exodus, the liberated children of Israel preferred the golden calf to the law from the mountain. In as imperious a way as the fundamentalists, the liberationists condemn any who have reservations about any social, political, or economic aspect of their message, especially if these reservations are rooted in a theology suspicious of historical dialectics as the clue to God's Kingdom. Further, in their zeal to affirm the dignity of the oppressed and in their prophetic efforts to achieve a measure of justice for them, they often attribute more virtue and wisdom to the dispossessed than human experience and justice itself warrant. Frequently they draw from Marxist forms of social analysis that not only distort the accurate understanding of the causes of oppression but also lean toward the romantic view that enforced dispossession purifies insight by unmasking every illusion. In fact, the poor are often embittered, enraged, full of illusion, stunted in perspective, and ignorant about political and economic causation. Sometimes they simply vent a vengeful fury in the name of a "totally new" reading of Scripture that destroys reason, compassion, the tissues of culture, and the capacity for disciplined theological, historical, and social reflections by which the lust for power, the cynical pursuit of interest, and viciousness are held in check.

In addition, by their emphasis on "liberation," liberationists imply that the chief issue in human life is too much heteronomous order, for which autonomous freedom is the cure. This enlightenment prescription may well describe part of the problem in some situations, but in many of the contexts for which liberationists speak, the central problem seems to be chaos and the autonomous, arbitrary power that pretends to contain it in the name of traditional authority, national security, or antisubversion.

Liberationists seldom inquire about what constructive patterns of political and economic life are required to structure complex modern societies. They so strongly stress protest against present patterns of life and the necessary uses of violence to bring the necessary change that they neglect reconstructive visions of a kind of social and institutional order that can constantly renew itself. Both their inattention to the normative resources for ordering the dynamism of modern societies and their tendency to see every social question solely in terms of power analysis leave liberationists prey to totalitarian tendencies. These limitations of contemporary liberationism prevent many would-be allies and supporters of its valid insights from taking it as seriously as its advocates would like.[2]

---

2. See Dennis McCann, *Christian Realism and Liberation Theology: Practical Theologies in Creative Conflict* (Maryknoll, N.Y.: Orbis Books, 1981); and Nicholas Wolterstorff, *Until Justice and Peace Embrace* (Grand Rapids: Eerdmans, 1983).

Despite the narrow dogmatism of much contemporary liberationism, its advocates do in fact know that any philosophy, social
science, or religious orientation that does not contain a substantial
measure of passion for social justice is fundamentally inadequate
from the perspective of a public theology. Sooner or later, the God
who finally governs history will bring those patterns of social change
that will rectify the oppressive patterns that have, for most of history over most of the globe, shattered the lives of simple people
and perpetuated their sad condition. Those who oppose these
changes by trying to array their religion against God's justice are
doomed. But these valid insights need to be placed in a larger
context of theological and social understanding. It is simply not
clear that all that has come and is coming out of modern revolutionary movements is "the Kingdom," or even that God's Kingdom
is to be fulfilled entirely on earth or in history. The greatest allies
of liberation movements may not be those who uncritically establish solidarity with them, but those who critically and carefully
attempt to marshal the philosophical, sociological, political-economic, and theological resources to put the movement's valid insights in a more sustainable and less ideological context.

VOCATION AND COVENANT

The third theme of considerable import for a public theology is
vocation. It rests on the view that the Creator God who also demands social engagement for justice in history has a purpose for
individuals and groups. Vocation is the answer to the question
"Why am I?" Everyone has a vocation from God that he or she may
choose to follow or ignore. From the calling of Abraham and Sarah,
through the calling of the prophets and the apostles, to the profound
sense of religious vocation in the Catholic monastic tradition and
the sense of the priesthood of all believers of the Reformation, the
idea that each of us is put into the world by God for a purpose and
called to serve the whole of life in the economy of God is a profound
and penetrating insight. It entails the belief that all of us are created
in the image of God and that each of us has a role to play in
fulfilling God's purpose. Vocation implies that the *chief end* of our
lives is to serve God through the actualization of the purposes for
which we were created. In what we do in all aspects of our lives,
especially in our work, we are not simply our own. We belong to
a reality that is greater than ourselves. This theme qualifies the
insights of the fundamentalists who press toward an enforced het-

eronomy and of the liberationists who celebrate autonomy, for we are called to theonomy.[3]

This highly personal notion has direct implications for public life. Those who are in positions of authority cannot lord it over others, for they are fundamentally in the service of purposes beyond their own. In addition, they are to assist the neighbor in finding, becoming equipped for, and living out his or her vocation. Further, if society at this or that stage of development is so designed that we or our neighbors are structurally prevented from becoming what we or they are called to be, then society is in error and must be changed. If women are called to the ministry and are not permitted to be ordained, God's purpose is frustrated. If workers who are willing and able to serve the public and support their families cannot find jobs; if minorities are called to participation and are excluded; if scientists, scholars, and writers are prevented from sharing their insights by constrictions on the freedom of the press — if any of these situations exists, something is wrong. Societies, cultures, and religions that hold people in thralldom and prevent actualization of their giftedness can be — indeed, must be — changed in a direction that will allow these people to become what God wants them to be, to do what God wants them to do.

The concept of vocation not only relates to our personal lives but has direct meanings for a multiplicity of public institutions as well. Putting the matter this way, to be sure, means that this concept of vocation bears within it a theological conviction about pluralism in society, one in which creation and history require multiple "spheres," "arenas," or "orders" of life. Each one must ask, "Why do we exist as a community?" Schools and colleges, courts of law and hospitals, art museums and research institutes, manufacturing corporations and labor unions, churches and legislatures — all have distinctive vocations. They are called to fulfill certain functions of and for humanity, and they must do so with excellence and clarity of purpose, or they are subject to either critique and transformation or destruction. If a university becomes a political party or a psychiatric center, if a corporation becomes a military camp or a charity organization, if a church becomes a museum or a court of law, it has betrayed its central vocation. Each sector of the common life

---

3. See *Theonomy and Autonomy: Studies in Paul Tillich's Engagement with Modern Culture,* ed. John J. Carey (Macon, Ga.: Mercer University Press, 1984).

is called by God to define, obey, and enhance the specific values and purposes that are proper to it.[4]

We have seen, in the not-so-distant past, how dangerous this idea of pluralistic social vocations can be if it is wrongly applied to tribes, clans, castes, races, or genders. It leads to forms of apartheid that deny the possibilities of personal vocation to those of the "wrong" genetic code. In the twentieth century we have also seen what happens when the different spheres of life are forced to follow values proper to another area. Totalitarian governments right and left have attempted to take control of the functions of all institutional sectors of society. When they succeed, education becomes propaganda, industry is militarized, law is politicized, art becomes ideology, and specific religions become law or are made illegal. The particular vocational tasks and professional values of each sector become obscure. The sense of service to the whole that each sector gets by doing particular things well on its own terms, thereby counterbalancing distortions elsewhere, gets lost.

Closely related to vocation is a fourth theme indispensable for a public theology: *covenant.* Covenant responds to the question of *how* we humans are to form communities of mutual responsibility as we live out our vocations. People require one another to be whole, and persons in community require a shared framework of common moral obligation that provides the principles by which to structure these relationships.

In the biblical tradition, covenant is seen as a gift of God that bonds the human will to God's justice and to the neighbor in structures of mutual accountability. Historically, "covenant" is the core of the prophetic tradition and has been in contention with two other major understandings of human relatedness — one patriarchal, the other contractual. In patriarchalism it is presumed that some by nature have the right and duty to dominate others in a universe that is inevitably hierarchical. One finds patriarchy in all caste societies, in some theories of marriage, and in many paternalistic condescensions of daily life. It is also frequent in fundamentalism. In contractualism it is presumed that there are no objective — and certainly no absolute — moral guidelines for ordering human rela-

---

4. See J. F. A. Taylor, *The Masks of Society: An Inquiry into the Covenants of Civilization* (East Norwalk, Conn.: Appleton-Century-Crofts, 1966); and Michael Walzer, *Spheres of Justice: A Defense of Pluralism and Equality* (Princeton: Princeton University Press, 1982).

tions. Thus humans construct religions, theologies, ethics, and social forms by acts of will and imagination alone. These artifacts of human creativity can be constantly renegotiated according to the desires and felt needs of the parties involved. At moments of disadvantage, agreements may be broken. This view is frequent in liberationism. If pursued, patriarchalism leads us to new feudalisms; contractualism, to arbitrary relativism.

Covenant recognizes the need for different levels of accountability in social relationships. It has structures of authority, but it calls leadership to regard, serve, and care for those in lower positions. Covenant also recognizes the role of voluntary choice and human agreement, but it sees the basic terms within which viable agreements are made as set by a higher law than we can fabricate out of arbitrary human will or calculate by the changing perceptions of advantage. In short, covenant holds that God sets forth terms and limits for our lives together, and that whatever authority we have and however we exercise our wills, we are to be subject to these terms. There are, as it were, objective mandates for living that require fidelity, obedience, and a willingness to live lovingly with those whom we at times cannot stand. Christians hold that particular covenants of our lives occur in a context that extends, finally, to all humanity, for we are bonded together in a mutuality of existence not of our own construction. Covenant is thus the community-ordering side of vocation.[5] It also leads us to the next indispensable motif: *moral law.*

MORAL LAW, SIN, AND FREEDOM

The idea that there is a law of God is a deep and profound insight that has nearly been lost in modern times. Perhaps because some interpretations of God's law have become so petty, legalistic, and self-righteous, or linked to patriarchalism, the idea itself has ceased to be compelling to many. Others have become so enamored with the Enlightenment views of human autonomy and absolute freedom that they give credence only to antinomian perceptions. Yet moral law attempts to answer the question, "Is there right and wrong?"

A public theology will hold that there are universally valid

---

5. See Joseph L. Allen, *Love and Conflict: A Covenantal Model of Christian Ethics* (Nashville: Abingdon, 1984).

moral laws rooted in God.[6] A common plumb line stands beyond all cultures, beyond all particular codes of civil laws and institutionalized rules. These laws are ethically valid whether or not they are observed in particular societies. Indeed, these laws become the basis for changing laws and rules when they are unjust. It is morally wrong to murder, rape, steal, torture, oppress, and enslave, whatever the cultural mores, the sociopolitical ideology, or the social needs of a given region, culture, community, or time.

Most of the Roman Catholic tradition and large segments of Protestantism — as well as a number of the non-Christian world religions — hold that there is a higher moral law, and that it can be known in some measure by human reason without special revelation. This is called "natural law." The term may be confusing because of the way our understanding of "nature" has been altered by modern science, but the point is integral to public theology. Indeed, whenever biblical politics, civil religions, or various spiritualities have become irrational, nontheological voices in philosophy, the (natural or social) sciences, or jurisprudence have corrected them by appeal to a universal, rational moral law. Public theology acknowledges such insights from these fields, includes them, and therefore remains constantly engaged in a broad interdisciplinary dialogue. Similarly, when a religion becomes purely confessional and bases its ethics on privileged insight, appeals to universal reasonability correct it. No one can say, "Sorry, I have never heard of the Ten Commandments revealed on Mount Sinai, and I am of another faith (or of no religion). Therefore, I shall proceed to exploit, murder, and expropriate according to my own beliefs." Baby Doc of Haiti, Pol Pot of Kampuchea, Idi Amin of Uganda, Ernesto Samoza of Nicaragua, and a dozen other figures or movements one could name have no such excuse.

We must acknowledge that for all the centuries of reflection on God's law and all the philosophies of "natural law," it remains very difficult to specify exactly what the moral laws are in the positive sense. To be sure, some seem rather clear: tell the truth, keep promises, defend the innocent. But the negative laws (no murder, no rape, no torture, no stealing, etc.) are much easier to define. This is so because the first question about moral law in public

---

6. See Boston Theological Institute, *Human Rights and the Global Mission of the Church,* Annual Series, 1985, vol. 1; and Robin Lovin, *Christian Faith and Public Choices: The Social Ethics of Barth, Brunner, and Bonhoeffer* (Philadelphia: Fortress Press, 1984).

theology is not whether we know what to say positively about what we ought to do at every point. The first question is whether we hold that there is a moral order in the universe that we can seek to know through dialogue and reflection. We may be able to discern only the negative limits with clarity. But that is no small matter. In the face of recent resurgences of barbarianism, it is such efforts as the United Nations' Declaration on Human Rights that manifest the possibility of clarifying a common, universal moral law to guide modern civilizations. This declaration does not tell every society how to structure its political economy, but it does define what ought not to be violated.[7]

The sixth theme pertinent to a public theology is implied in all the previous principles: *sin*. Reinhold Niebuhr once argued that this is the most empirical doctrine in the panoply of Christian doctrines.[8] Any who do not believe that sin is a reality in the world need only look around. We believe that God is sovereign over creation and history, and that humans have a vocation — both individually and in association with each other — to serve, to covenant together in community, and to obey the moral law. But it is also the case that we encounter distortion, brokenness, corruption, and failure within ourselves and in every sociohistorical context. We humans are beset by the constant temptation to betray ourselves, our neighbors, our callings, our covenants, the moral law, and God. We can always find social movements and tendencies within the self that are hell-bent on destruction, and we perennially ask why. Sin is the generic answer.

Sin is, of course, impossible without the seventh theme: *freedom*. Human freedom is the answer to the question of how sin entered the world if God created it. A public theology will acknowledge that freedom as a gift of God is both the mark of being genuinely human and the occasion for licentiousness and betrayal. Presumably, God could so order the universe that perfect harmony would be the result. But that would entail the denial of choice. Various regimes in family or political life, in academia or the workplace sometimes attempt what God could have done but did not

---

7. See Walter Harrelson, *The Ten Commandments and Human Rights*, ed. Walter Brueggemann and John Donahue (Philadelphia: Fortress Press, 1980); and Kosuke Koyama, *Mount Fuji and Mount Sinai: A Critique of Idols* (Maryknoll, N.Y.: Orbis Books, 1984).

8. Niebuhr, *The Nature and Destiny of Man*, 2 vols. (New York: Scribner's, 1939).

do: to so regulate everything that friction or breakdown, conflict or failure cannot occur. But while efficient engineering and management may well be a virtue in certain material operations, it is not so in all aspects of human existence. A God who leaves no place for error, contrition, and free choosing of what is right and good is not a God who can touch the core of human existence, just as no social arrangement that destroys freedom in a totally regulated environment can sustain human loyalty.

A public theology marks the delicate relationship of freedom and sin by making a rather sharp distinction between sin and crime. Not all things that are sinful should be seen as crimes. Public authorities are not competent to evaluate a wide range of sins, and governments must exercise great restraint at this point. The only government deemed valid by a public theology will be a limited government. It will allow the "social space" for freedom—and risk the perils of sin in many areas of religion, the arts, family life, science, and economic activity. Thus a public theology will resist any clerical experts on creation or liberation or moral law who attempt to effect total control of cultural, social, political, or economic life. Instead, a public theology will always work indirectly. It will attempt to persuade people to exercise their cultural, social, political, and economic freedom responsibly through pluralistic institutions, allowing governments to constrict those public behaviors that are a clear threat to human rights or the common good and that cannot be controlled by other means.

ECCLESIOLOGY AND TRINITY

This concern is intimately linked to the next motif: *ecclesiology.* This involves the question of how those who know themselves to be sinners and to be constantly tempted to use their freedom in destructive ways, and yet who know something about the Creator and liberating God who calls us to vocation and covenant under a moral law, are to organize their life together and forward their views in the public domain. A focus on ecclesiology demands the institutional separation of church and state, and the simultaneous claim of the right of religious groups to propagate their views on public affairs among the people. The separation of church and state does not mean the segregation of theology from public life and from the attempt to guide political and economic life through persuasion, preaching, and teaching. Indeed, such separation makes it possible to form nonestablished groups who will selectively embrace or repudiate the structures, tendencies, programs, values, and actions of public figures and institutions. This legacy of the "free church" tradition is widely accepted among Christian "magisterial" religious traditions today, and it has also made modern societies safe for the Jewish synagogue, the Muslim mosque, the Hindu temple, the Buddhist center, and the humanist cell. In such an environment, conversions to new views of God, humanity, and the world are to be expected.

Another dimension of this accent on ecclesiology is that our primary "reference group" cannot be nation or state, tribe or clan, economic organization or class. The frail connective tissues of belief and ethics that connect us through ecclesial organizations to peoples of all nations, races, and economic groups are more significant for our basic value structures than even the families, political systems, and economic institutions in which we spend most of our time and properly invest much of our psychic and physical energy. For all their faults and foibles, organized religion, the church, ecumenical institutions, and transcultural, interfaith centers of dialogue and encounter are the living witnesses to those human attempts to clarify godly meanings that give life structure and purpose beyond our "interests." When one compares the empirical ecclesial bodies to what they could and should be, the results are inevitably discouraging. Only when they are compared with the rest of human social existence can their significance for complex societies be sensed and the cosmopolitan scope of their concerns be identified.[9]

Implicit here is a certain, if modest, confidence in persuasion — in a way of witnessing and giving testimony to what is believed that demands reasonable discourse and warranted authority, with the corollary that those who are not persuaded need not be compelled to join. In fact, use of coercion in the establishment or the suppression of religious groups and principles leads to a lie in the soul that destroys the human fabric on which every public order must stand. Ecclesiology presumes that noncoercive communities of discourse are the core communities of civilization, for here the Word may be freely refined or elaborated and connected to familial, political, and economic existence as well as personal existence.

But persuasion is not all discursive and conceptual. Much of it is aesthetic and symbolic. And the formation of every ecclesial group requires the development of liturgical, ritual, and graceful

---

9. See my *Ethics and the Urban Ethos* (Boston: Beacon Press, 1973).

forms of shared experience. At their worst, these may become magical; frequently, they become merely ceremonial. But at their deepest, they may become sacramental. They celebrate the truth and justice of God known in the community of faith, and communicate by ordered communal drama a theological vision of how the created order is related to the grace of God, to the destiny that God intends for life, and to the present responsibilities of humans in relationship to nature, each other, and society. The symbolic character of such rites is inevitably multileveled, and thus allows humans to relate multiple and complex variables in sacred unities of meaning. The stewardship of such rites, by careful attention to their rich complexity, becomes the paradigm of human communication and respect for institutional integrity.

The modern ecumenical movement, with its roots largely in the Protestant Reformation, has not paid much attention to the role of liturgy, ritual, sacred drama, and sacrament in public life. We have been little prepared to face the influence that liturgized forms of shared experience have in political and economic life, and many of our most influential traditions have failed to draw upon the rich resources of sacramental tradition to guide our attitudes about political and economic life. Yet for many — all over the world, in many traditions — religion is essentially about symbolic actions rightly performed. That is how and where people get their sense of propriety, legitimacy, and authority for human relationships and social institutions. A public theology will attend to sacramental sensibilities and critically evaluate their capacity to inform the common life. They are indispensable to ecclesiology.

A key doctrinal example of multileveled meaning is the Christian understanding of the *Trinity,* the ninth key motif in a public theology. In the classical formation of this doctrine, it was established that both the inner life of God (insofar as humans could know anything about it) and the ways in which God relates to the world involve pluralism and unity. In sharp protest against every monolithic view of reality and in contrast to every polytheism, the doctrine of the Trinity conceives of ultimate reality in terms of a coherent, integrated diversity. It is a summary statement of the conviction that the ultimate reality which created the world and which finally governs history is made up of persons with specific vocations inextricably bound together in covenantal community, cosmic in scope.

The doctrine of the Trinity also recognizes that at certain points, a secondary dualism has to be acknowledged. This can most clearly be seen in the doctrine of the "two natures" of Christ, but it is pertinent to the other persons of the Trinity also. The point is that a radical appreciation of transcendence and a radical appreciation of the human are both true but are not the same, and neither may be reduced to the other.

To be sure, the doctrine of the Trinity is the most distinctive doctrine of Christianity, and one of the key insights that distinguishes the theology of this tradition from those religions with which Christianity may be, in other ways, closely allied — Judaism, Islam, and theistic Hinduism. In some ways, therefore, this is a very difficult doctrine to defend in public discourse. Yet, as we shall see, it may be that precisely this doctrine is also indispensable to the formation of a viable public theology.

All this implies that ecumenically oriented churches are those best suited to nurture and propagate a public theology, and that they have to make the case for what they believe by carrying their message to the population — person by person, group by group — and run the risk that it may be modified as it is filtered through the consciences of the people in reasonable dialogue and as it encounters the inevitable demands of complex civilizational life. To put it another way, the ecumenical perspectives on a public theology must be "evangelical" in order to become reformed and catholic, and must be catholic and constantly reforming to become public. But a public theology will constantly take as its base points key "orthodox" motifs from Scripture, Tradition, Reason, and Experience. This will involve the willingness to join and meet all the objections, resistances, and oppositions that one can possibly imagine from a generation that is religiously confused, philosophically undernourished, socially divided, and theologically illiterate. A public theology has to make its case in an open market of ideas among the people, and to develop those patterns of sacramental action by which the truth and justice of God are symbolized in community. To this end, adult theological education is likely to be the most important task of religious organizations in the foreseeable future. Both our ecclesiastical structures and our training of church leadership must reflect that demand. Public life must be so structured as to allow the free exercise of religion in these senses. No other cluster of institutions can do what is required.

I believe that the motifs I have outlined form the public theological matrix of intellectual, ethical, spiritual foci for stewardship and the group of chief themes of which we are to be stewards. This is the

"Word" that we are called to clarify, to celebrate, to refine, to defend, to propagate in public discourse, to incarnate in social and institutional life, and to contextualize amid the complexities of modern political economies.

And here we may state overtly what has already been implied throughout this chapter. Such motifs not only clarify and communicate something of the truth and justice of God, but also drive all who begin to wrestle with the meanings of such themes into social analysis and social engagement. Such notions have a peculiar status in conceptual life: they simultaneously are normative and demand contextual encounter with life as it is. That is, they not only convey something of the truth and justice of God, which are always beyond human affairs, but they have a component that connects particular social and historical possibilities within the realm of human affairs. Indeed, they demand a certain discernment of particular possibilities, sometimes known only in fragments and hints, that illuminate the whole. They allow us to recognize where, in the plethora of thoughts, experiences, and behaviors, the traces of the transcendent may be found; and they invite us to build, by transformative action, new possibilities on these real if fragile foundations.

How such motifs as these have guided Christians during the last century, when modern political economies have developed most rapidly under the impact of industrialization, is the subject to which we next turn. These modern adaptations of the themes may give us certain clues as to how we might reconstruct a public theology in the midst of new transitions to a "postindustrial," high-tech, and increasingly global and professionalized society.

Study Questions

A Christian public theology is guided not only by touchstones of authority but also by specific themes or principles that are thought to be indispensable to Christian witness in the world. The nine principles explored in this chapter are:

Creation	Covenant	Religious Freedom
Liberation	Moral Law	Ecclesiology
Vocation	Sin	Trinity

1. Each principle is designed to answer a particular question about life and the world. What are the questions that Christians believe these principles answer? Do you think everyone asks these questions? Do you?

2. If these principles are based in Scripture, rooted in Tradition,

marked by Reason, and informed by Experience, do they influence our personal faith? Do they influence our thought about public matters? Should they?

3. Does fundamentalism contradict any of these themes? Why? What difference does it make in public life?

4. Does liberationism contradict any of these themes? Why? What difference does it make in public life?

5. Do "vocation" and "profession" differ? Can an organization or an institution have a vocation?

6. How can we distinguish between sin and crime? Does this distinction make any difference in our views of sexual, political, and economic ethics?

7. Should the church challenge creationism? Evolution? Is there a better way of understanding the relation of Scripture and modern science?

8. What is the difference between covenant and contract in marriage, business, and politics?

9. Do you believe that there is a "universal moral law," even if different cultures have different ethical rules, different religions teach different morals, and different governments have different laws? What are the implications for some kind of consensus necessary in public affairs?

10. Do you believe in the freedom of religion? Do you think that "Moonies" and various cults should be free to convert people? Do you think that groups such as Roman Catholics, "T.V. fundamentalists," liberationists, and the National Council of Churches ought be allowed to influence the media, the public schools, and legislation?

11. How does the church's involvement/non-involvement in social matters impinge upon the stewardship of the Word? How does your understanding of the Word lead you to involvement or non-involvement in social matters?

12. To what extent has sacramentalism become purely ornamental in your congregation? Who is responsible for the stewardship of liturgy, ritual, sacrament, and Word in public life?

13. Sometimes the church does not lead the struggles for creative social change. Sometimes the methods and goals of social change seem opposed to Christian doctrine. How is Christian witness affected by such situations?

CHAPTER THREE

The Roots of Christian Sociology

In the last chapter, we spoke of ten themes indispensable to a public theology but dealt with only nine. Although we hinted at the tenth, Christology, we did not debate it. It is the theme that is most debatable and that in the deep tradition has seldom been related to political economics in a very direct way. In the next two chapters we will see that, in fact, very serious reflection on precisely these matters has taken place for more than a century. Decisive in the extension and revision of Tradition on this front has been the formation of a "Christian sociology." It represents the development of some very critical themes for a Christian public theology in the face of modern political economies. I want to recall this tradition because it specifically combined the motifs already discussed in a new way, because it puts part of our present malaise in some perspective, and because it represents a significant extension of *tradition* that attempted to work with *Scripture* in a *reasonable* way to address contemporary *experience* in an increasingly industrialized society.

In the nineteenth century, the full force of the Industrial Revolution was felt beyond England and came to grand visibility on the Continent, where before it had developed slowly. It belatedly engulfed America under the stimulus of the Civil War, and through commerce, education, and especially European colonialism, it penetrated every corner of the globe. Yet within five decades the "open frontiers" in North America, Africa, and South America began to close. Henceforth, economic development would occur by intensification of the technological means of extraction, production, and distribution, and through the expansion of the corporation centered in the city rather than by expansion of territory and the exertions of settlers bringing virgin lands under the plow with the involuntary help of "native" peoples. Traditional economies and the long-standing patterning of the classes based on them were eroded or exploded by these developments. And increasingly, such economic developments were dealt with by the emerging social sciences, by new, nonreligious forms of moral reflection, and by industrial planners on grounds first cultivated by the intellectuals of several ideological stripes who had broken the connections between political theory and economics on the one hand and religious ethics on the other.

But theologians were not about to allow nonreligious or antireligious orientations to define the future. That path, they believed, always led to chaos or to tyranny. Early leaders selectively utilized the new secular theorists but subordinated their governing insights to recovered and recast biblical and traditional principles. In so doing they showed the continued pertinence of theology to public affairs under contemporary conditions.

THE FIGHT AGAINST SLAVERY

The most important single factor that transformed modern theological attitudes toward the political economy was the evangelical drive against slavery. Timothy Smith's highly regarded *Revivalism and Social Reform* shows that the roots of the modern reexamination of economic ethics are in the American revivals of the pre–Civil War period.[1] Some branches of the older Calvinism, which had dominated earlier theologies of economics, had begun to petrify. The newer movements claimed to be more closely related to what the gospel, the early church, and the Reformation had been about. Although doctrinal disputes preoccupied much revivalistic attention — specifically regarding the new threats of Unitarianism on the one hand and Arminianism on the other — the social debates focused on the questions of property, work, and wealth as matters of Christian stewardship and outward manifestations of obedience to Christ.

Earlier Calvinism had entered into a somewhat uncomforta-

---

1. Smith, *Revivalism and Social Reform* (New York: Harper & Row, 1957). See also George Marsden, *Fundamentalism and American Culture: The Shaping of Twentieth Century Evangelicalism* (New York: Oxford University Press, 1980).

ble alliance with philosophical modes of thought from the English Enlightenment, particularly those of Locke. This alliance produced both new shapes of democratic constitutional government and certain understandings of human rights, but also an interpretation of private property that was nearly absolute. Locke had argued that the three "natural rights" of individuals were life, liberty, and property. But both the Calvinists of New England and the drafters of the American Declaration of Independence had already modulated that formulary both by challenging Locke's radical individualism and by proclaiming that humans are "endowed by their Creator with certain unalienable Rights, that among these are Life, Liberty and the pursuit of Happiness." This shift is all the more remarkable because it occurred just as the work of Adam Smith was being published.

However, it was not until the antebellum revival movements that the absoluteness of private property rights was challenged in substance. Then the question was posed sharply: Can Christians hold other people in slavery as property, and can a public policy that allows this be allowed to survive? From 1840 on, revivals were held from Boston to Iowa City that included powerful preaching against slavery and the individualistic doctrines of property that enslaved human souls. Dozens of books and hundreds of articles grew out of this movement, pitting "the principles of Jesus" against slavery. The authors virtually dared Southern theologians to try to prove the evangelical righteousness of their system by Scripture or Reason, as several were inclined to do.

Since there is evidence of slavery in the Bible, a weighty question was soon brought to the forefront of the discussion: Which parts of the Bible are normative for all times, and which parts reflect the temporal outlook of a particular period of history? To ask this question is to open the door to a historical interpretation of Scripture. The question also invites the analysis of present historical conditions in comparison with the ancient ones. It opens the way for a new discernment of the principles from Scripture because the experience of new social conditions and deeper understandings of reason forces new questions that previous ages may not have encountered. It leads to fresh applications of newly discerned principles to changing conditions. Indeed, it makes the synthesizing of biblically based ethical principles with continuously modified social analysis an ongoing task that forms new traditions.

If authors of this period did not quite accept Ranke's aphorism that "Every age is immediate to God," they did accept the idea that there are "epochs" in human history and that each age has its own vocation under God. Each generation must renew the covenants of society in new ways under God's universal moral law. Among the antislavery evangelicals, this idea led to the view that the challenge of this particular age was on the social-economic front, especially vis-à-vis the crisis of slavery and the new shapes of industrial life. Many believed (as others were to articulate more fully in the next generation) that under the impact of Christian theology and ethics, political life was being democratized, legal institutions had established equality as a governing principle even where it was inequitably applied, "modern" education was making accessible to many what had once been the privilege of a few, and patriarchal authoritarianism in family life had been abolished as a moral norm if not as a fact. But now, under the influence of both the old plantation systems and the new "robber barons" of the industrializing era, a new, exploitative cluster of elites was on the rise and threatening the gains that had been made in these other areas of life. Rich families, centered in notable households and passing their wealth and privilege from father to son, were consolidating political power and economic influence in ways that echoed the feudal hierarchies thought to have been left behind. Such was the challenge of these days, of this epoch.

Once the door was open to challenge the doctrine of the absolute rights of property, both secular Enlightenment theories of property (in the tradition of Locke) and decadent theories of Calvinism (which saw personal wealth as a sign of special divine favor) came under increased criticism.

A further word needs to be said about this relationship with Calvinism before we proceed further. Calvinism had shaped the main contours of American religion in all its previous history, and had drawn on the warrants for authority and most of the motifs for a public theology mentioned in the preceding chapters. But this tradition split into three increasingly distinct branches. One branch, as Anne Douglas has artfully demonstrated, was "feminized" — an unfortunate choice of terms for an essentially correct argument.[2] This pietistic branch became almost totally preoccupied with the cultivation of the "gentler virtues" and the manicuring of the inner religious sensibilities. It lost its concern for public matters. Another

---

2. Douglas, *The Feminization of American Culture* (New York: Avon Press, 1978). Compare E. D. Baltzell, *Puritan Boston and Quaker Philadelphia* (New York: The Free Press, 1979).

branch became the bastion of antiscientific fideism, the forerunner of a literalistic fundamentalism that turned parts of Christianity toward a "Koranized" biblicism accenting the complete verbal inspiration of the Bible.

The third branch, however, is one that could be called "Protestant-evangelical." It consisted of those denominations that later became the core of the ecumenical movement of the twentieth century. They claimed to be the heirs of the truly catholic church, the Reformation, and the Puritan traditions. They became the advocates of a new economic ethic. It is these denominations that James Dombrowski has in mind when he writes that those who had a manifest interest in social and economic questions "had a correlative existence with Calvinism. It showed its greatest strength in . . . [those places] where Calvinism was most deeply entrenched. Thus, to some extent, the 'this worldly' emphasis of Calvinism produced a social Christianity opposed to the 'other worldliness' of Lutheranism and the 'next worldliness' of Catholicism [in this period]. Withdrawal from the world . . . was rejected in favor of participation in the world with a view to transforming it."[3] This perspective was shared by Methodists, Low Church Anglicans, Baptists, and believers from a host of the newer American denominations, even if they self-consciously broke with certain doctrinal accents in Calvinism.

In any case, the door of criticism was being pried open. In 1851, Stephen Colwell, a Presbyterian trustee of Princeton Theological Seminary, wrote *New Themes for the Protestant Clergy.* Published only three years after the *Communist Manifesto* but more dependent on evolutionary thought than revolutionary socialist thought, this little volume argued that "the whole socialist movement . . . [is] one of the greatest events of this age. . . . The works of socialists have exposed this hideous skeleton of selfishness — they have pursued it with unfaltering hatred; and this constitutes our main obligation to them." Such an unveiling of the soft underbelly of industrial prosperity, Colwell argued, was to be met by a new application of Christian principles — stewardship, fellowship, compassion, justice, and honesty — to the economic order. Not only must slavery be abolished, but the emerging "wage slavery" of the new industries must be challenged before it became entrenched.

Slavery — under the combined pressure of Christian business

---

3. Dombrowski, *The Early Days of Christian Socialism in America* (New York: Octagon Books, 1966), p. 15.

influence from the North, populist evangelical zeal, and internal pressures from the slave community itself — was legally abolished within a generation, but both the political economic status of newly freed blacks and the "wage slavery" that held many more in bondage were only slowly challenged. Colwell had anticipated the flood of criticism that was to flow soon after the Civil War, in part because this war itself drew more and more people into the rapid industrialism it triggered. New cycles of boom and bust, new relationships of labor and owners, and new concentrations of wealth transformed the dreams of yeoman farmers from crops and neighbors to the realities of factories and unions.

THE REJECTION OF
"THE BLOODY LAW OF TOOTH AND CLAW"

Because we sometimes remember the frontier days of the wild West as typical of the post–Civil War years, we forget that the cities were growing faster than the frontier. Between 1860 and 1890 the urban population quadrupled, while the rural population only doubled. The industrial city took supreme command, and that meant factories, technology, trade, commerce, corporations, and labor and service industries. It also meant enormous increases in governmental involvement in economic life — building roads and streets, expanding police forces, putting in sewers and streetlights, and regulating patents, zoning, and transportation. In 1776, only about three percent of the population of the United States was urban, and the rest was engaged in agriculture. Today, because of post–Civil War changes, only about three percent of the population is involved in agriculture, and that number is declining as agriculture itself is increasingly controlled by "agribusiness" corporations. No other economic transformation in human history has been as rapid, as pervasive, or as socially transformative.

Parallel to these dramatic changes, theory was also changing. The ideas of Adam Smith were frequently wedded to the new theories of social Darwinism. The very laws of nature seemed to endorse "the survival of the fittest" and "the bloody law of tooth and claw." But this is precisely what was challenged by the clergy. They increasingly rejected the presuppositions of this form of laissez-faire economics. In a highly significant study of this period, C. H. Hopkins notes that "they regarded unrestricted competition as an arrogant contradiction of Christian ethics and the unhuman treatment accorded the laborer as a violation of the fundamental Protestant conceptions of the nature of man."[4] In 1866 the Reverend G. H. Boardman saw an affront both to Christian principles and to good science in Adam Smith's theory that individualism and selfishness could produce good results if only the providential laws of the market were given free rein. Two years later, the Reverend John Bascom of Williams College argued that the logic of Smith's work would lead to the polarization and fixation of class divisions.

Scattered sermons, periodical essays, and whole journals began to wrestle with these issues. Lyman Atwater's essay of 1872, "The Labor Question and Its Economic and Christian Aspects," was widely quoted for years. He argued for profit sharing and claimed that the industrialist "is bound by every Christian and moral obligation to give the laborer a fair and righteous share of the rewards of production." And, as C. H. Hopkins points out, Joseph Cook of Boston, Richard Newton of New York, and dozens of lesser known writers were arguing the same themes in the *Methodist Quarterly Review,* the *Baptist Standard,* and the *Sunday Afternoon.*

These efforts were fed by European writings. In 1865 Sir John Robert Seeley published *Ecce Homo,* a work widely read and reviewed in America. He argued that the true meaning of Jesus was to be found in his purpose for the church, and the purpose of the church was the improvement of social morality. John Ruskin's *Unto This Last* (1862) had an even more pronounced influence. In this work, filled with invective against the modern economic system, he prescribed a return to the golden age of agrarian harmony with nature as God intended. This work was quoted for nearly half a century and has had an impact on subsequent thinkers from Mahatma Gandhi to E. F. Schumacher, the author of the much-discussed *Small Is Beautiful* (1973). In his account of the development of these socioeconomic themes in American Christian thought, however, Francis Greenwood Peabody, the first professor of Christian social ethics in this land, pointed out that "by a strange perversion . . . [the] prophetic denunciations have outlived [the] positive teachings." Similar treatment would soon be accorded Frederick

---

4. Hopkins, *The Rise of the Social Gospel in American Protestantism: 1865-1915* (New Haven: Yale University Press, 1940). For my own more fully documented treatment of this period, see "Jesus and Economics," in *The Bible in American Law, Politics, and Political Rhetoric,* ed. James T. Johnson (Chico, Calif.: Scholars Press, 1985), pp. 107-51.

Maurice and Charles Kingsley as these two celebrated Christian Fabians became major leaders on the British scene.

German radical Christians were also widely quoted. From the revolution of 1848 on, a series of voices attempted to apply "the principles of Jesus" to economic matters. Rudolf Todt, Pastor Stoecker, and later Martin von Nathusius, Hermann Kuetter, and the Swiss-German Leonhard Ragaz became deeply involved in seeking the bases for a Christian interpretation of the economic issues of the day, often with specific reference to Marxist thought as it was developing among the laboring classes of Europe. Their efforts resulted in the formation, by 1889, of the Evangelical Social Congress, which was to sponsor yearly international conferences on Christianity and social issues. They drew into the circle leading figures from France and Italy who shared comparable concerns. It was in some ways the Christian effort to form a Christian, democratic "Non-Marxist International" committed to social change and economic justice. They knew that political-economic life had come to a great turning point. The era of feudalism had been defeated by the age of individualism, but the age of individualism itself had come to an end. Neither the prophets who had called for individualism nor those who demanded a return to older organic solidarities of "natural communitarianism" offered a theory that would suffice. A revitalized Christian ethic related to the new forms of social organization was needed.

THE AFFIRMATION OF
"CHRIST TRANSFORMING CULTURE"

Near the end of the nineteenth century, a large number of major figures were pursuing analogous courses in America. Washington Gladden, a nationally famous pastor and the president of the Missionary Society; Richard T. Ely, who founded the American Economic Association; W. D. P. Bliss, who edited the famous *Encyclopedia of Social Reform* — these and literally scores of other figures were able to publish hundreds of books that focused primarily on the transformation of the economy on the basis of a new social application of Jesus' message, specifically as it provided clues to the moral transformation of institutional life in modern society.

While the newer social sciences provided the analysis of the empirical situation, a distinctive understanding of the teachings and principles of Jesus provided the normative orientation. In continuity with Scripture and the classical teachings of the tradition,

Jesus was viewed as the *logos* of creation, as the crucified and resurrected Lord, as the source of the historically imminent power of the Kingdom of God, as the renewer of God's covenant, and as the Son of God. But Jesus was also seen as the initiator of a new era of social relations, one that challenges the principalities and powers that tend to rule every society. Yet Jesus was not only seen as one who offered criticism of the status quo; he was also seen as one who gave clues to new, constructive possibilities. In this regard, these transformers of tradition were "post-Protestant." They were above all "reconstructionist." They may well have been too optimistic, as they are often accused of being, but they refused to understand Christianity as a negation. Christ was not against culture; Christ transformed culture. And the task of modernity was first and foremost to identify the forms of grace and the dynamic spirit that could encounter the new world on the horizon and selectively embrace and reconstruct it.

On such foundations, one finds a rather wide spectrum of positions that have been advocated by particular authors and in church materials. These served as bases for both advocacy movements and scholarly work in "social Christianity," carried out under the titles of Christian Socialism, the Social Gospel, Religion and Labor, Christianity and Economics, Christianity and Industry, the Ethics of Wealth, Applied Christianity, and so forth. Indeed, by 1900 the body of literature under these and related headings had reached such proportions in the United States that the Library of Congress introduced the term "Christian Sociology" as a major heading to include these topics in its cataloguing system.

The common starting point was the crisis of the age, the experienced disjunctions of life. But the various proponents of this view not only condemned such disjunctions but wanted to infuse the evils of the age with a purpose that could reconstitute life in a positive direction. To guide the people of God in this crisis, these advocates turned to biblical and theological sources for social and ethical resources. They were alert to the new modes of biblical scholarship, and they also knew the work being done in church history and systematics. But such efforts were appropriated primarily as they helped to provide resources for the articulation and application of ethical principles to the social situation in which the people in the pews found themselves so that they could find their future in reconstructed possibilities.

By the beginning of the twentieth century, much that had been developed in more scattered efforts could be stated in less ad hoc fashion. Indeed, we can summarize these views in two ways. In the remainder of this chapter I will offer an overview of the major themes and accents of this emerging tradition. In the next chapter I will illustrate the spectrum of opinion that was worked out on those foundations and within which most of the writers for the next half century can be placed.

THE EMERGING THEMES OF "SOCIAL CHRISTIANITY"

The primary moral response to the rapid industrialization during this period was made by applying "the teachings of Jesus" to economic structures. But what our forebears smuggled in under the term was also freighted with Tradition, Reason, and Experience in a quest for a public theology. This is to say that other ethical resources were brought to bear on the crises experienced. Indeed, many aspects of the classical theory of natural law were utilized, as was material from the prophets of the Old Testament. Further, normative concepts were drawn from both medieval and Reformation theology. Still, both particular biblical texts and frequently repeated themes from the Synoptic Gospels were, more than any other single set of resources, the core of the modern, Western religious-ethical perspective on economic life.

As we will see, different authors drew on different biblical materials and wedded the results to economic life in different ways. Some turned to Jesus because they advocated a Christian engagement with economics out of a pastoral concern for those believers victimized by the raw edges of the new economic systems. Others, following the earlier traditions of Locke, believed that what could be worked out philosophically as the moral basis for political economy was best grasped by those who had neither the leisure nor the learning for sustained reflection if they but accepted the sublime ethical principles of Jesus. In some versions, the Continental rather than the Anglo-American Enlightenment was taken as the model of interpretation. Following the lead of the nineteenth-century neo-Kantians, some agreed with such authors as Adolph von Harnack and Rudolph Herrmann, who tended to see Kant's universalistic, formal principles everywhere in the teachings of Jesus. Still others saw in the quests for the historical Jesus the recovery of the most authentic and revolutionary message the world has ever known, which the church tradition with all its dogmas had long obscured. This accent led to a vision of the Kingdom of God that entailed progress toward a shared abundance of material resources in a cooperative New Jerusalem for all.

It is surely not unimportant in this connection that a profoundly personal pietism had tended to dominate in the immediately preceding period of Western religious life. The predominance of Lutheran Pietism in Germany, of populist evangelicalism in England, and of evangelistic revivalism on the American frontier had all pressed Protestantism toward an individualism that had challenged previous Christian thought and needed challenging itself in view of the new social complexities the faith was facing. Those who became engaged in moral reflection about economics knew that new, massive, modern structures had emerged in the "Christian West," and that they had been at least partially prompted by Protestant branches of Christianity in particular. These branches had a very high estimate of the continued import of the individual, but frequently the importance of the individual was focused on ultimate life in heaven. A decision for Christ made all the difference for the life to come. At the same time, the evangelical accent itself seemed to press converts to allow Christ to rule over all aspects of their earthly lives. And this was the point on which this movement built. It accented the notion that not only heaven but earth depended upon deciding for Christ and subsequently putting Jesus' principles into effective practice in the common institutions of life as well as in the soul. Sooner or later, modern social developments, including political and economic orientations and structures, had to be shown to be compatible or incompatible with God's purposes as known in Jesus Christ by the hearts of believers.

The turn to the New Testament entailed two rejections and one limitation that give a common stamp to the whole body of this American literature on economics. First, "possessive individualism" of the sort celebrated by those following the lead of Adam Smith was rejected. Perceiving the human creature as merely a rational calculator of costs and benefits does not fit with the New Testament message. And understanding society in terms of the automatic harmonies resulting from the efficient pursuit of private interests does not fit with a Christian interpretation of society. These perspectives fail to understand that sin — unless contained by repentance, justification, and sanctification, which bring people to obedience — deflects the rational capacities when interests are at stake. Further, egocentrism and concentrated power, which are the ordinary hallmarks of human societies, destroy social harmony. Only God can bring that transformation of the will that inclines people to see the import of compassion and that inclines societies to build an ethos by which vocation, covenant, and moral law are honored and actualized.

On another level, the evangelical founders of "social Christianity" argued that the predominant secular theories that were used to defend varieties of corporation-building did not empirically reflect how people lived and acted. The individualism of conservative capitalist theory was an abstraction of the worst sort. The great limited-liability corporations were not individualistic at all but new social organisms that had to be understood in social terms, even if they were headed by notable entrepreneurs. But this argument was not only empirical. The teachings of Jesus led the critics of the industrial barons and their philosophies to have a very high regard for individuals but a deep suspicion of individualism. Christians understood that all humans are joiners; they are members of communities and must be responsible in communities. People do not live in isolation on earth, in the church, or in heaven, and it is a lie to say they do or ought to in economic life. Only in hell is individualism real.

Similarly, atheistic and antireligious collectivism was rejected. Frequently this entailed explicit repudiation of the techniques, the ideology, and the nationalistic solidarity of a "civic religion," as well as the rejection of the violence of the French Revolution. As Protestants had burned the books of Rousseau in the streets of Geneva when he advocated a "totalistic" society, so the new advocates of "social Christianity" rejected the totalistic "sciences" of Comte and Marx, just as in the twentieth century they were to reject Lenin and Hitler even more strongly. The "secular," "materialist" perspectives that these figures represent were viewed as anti-God, anti-church, and destructive of a Christian respect for individuals. In each case, a vision of a "natural" group (nation, class, or race) was thought to be the clue to the political-economic future of humanity. What these "sciences" embraced were in fact false faiths that would inevitably rethrone tyranny in the name of "the people." The founding figures of "Christian sociology" had profound populist sympathies: most were quite patriotic and committed to working with the laboring classes. But most held that collectivism, whether defended on romantic or "scientific" grounds, was a threat to truth and justice, to pluralism and democracy, to humanity and the faith. The point was made in a thousand ways that collectivism does not comport with what Jesus taught or with the prudent stewardship of society or material creation; it brings only hell on earth in the name of emancipation.

In brief, the founders of modern "social Christianity" — whatever they drew indirectly from Adam Smith, Karl Marx, or their heirs — finally and fundamentally rejected the secular models of both individualistic, commercial capitalism and the collectivist political economy of communism. One of the main reasons they rejected these views is that both rest on an interpretation of *homo economicus* that sees humanity as basically driven by material interests, rationally calculated. While accepting this insight as a partially accurate empirical truth, theologians and ethicists of the Christian community repudiated it on both normative and descriptive grounds. Christians saw the power of this reality as a testimony to the reality of sin, which is always a possibility, given human freedom. But sin is not the final or the only influence in human affairs. In fact, said the founders of "social Christianity," people are and ought to be driven by cultural norms and religious values as much as by material interest, and to ignore this fact is both intellectually dishonest and morally repugnant. Loyalty to cultural norms and religious values, when they are properly ordered, is as rational as calculation of gains and losses. Thus the nature and character of predominant norms and values are of paramount importance. They offer clues to a reality beyond the fact of sin.

Drawing on biblical resources, Christian theologians and ethicists also pointed out a limitation of their creed. They argued that, while Christian ethics is necessary to sound economics, there are economic questions of a purely technical sort that cannot be answered by any biblically based perspective. They were well aware of problems that had developed earlier in the relations between theology and ethics on the one hand and the natural sciences on the other. These problems in Christian history arose whenever the ancient divines attempted to prescribe the contours of scientific work on the basis of religious and ethical doctrines alone, or attempted to construct normative views of truth and justice on descriptive interpretations of particular natural or historical events. They were not about to repeat these same errors in the newer social sciences, particularly economics.

It is not easy to move from "ought" to "is" or from "is" to "ought." Particular prescriptions for any policy are always synthetic. They always involve what later scholars call "middle axioms" — general guidelines for action that are subject to change if it is shown that the "is" is wrongly described, or that the first principles of "ought" are misunderstood. Thus one seldom finds detailed discussions of technical economic questions such as would be proper, for example, in a university course on economic measurements. Instead, one finds most treatments of economics set in the context of a more general interpretation of society. The focus is on Christian principles applied to the logic of social relations, of which one aspect is economics. The purpose is to clarify normative principles and general ends of economic activity, leaving considerable room for specific technical questions in economic thought and action.

Finally, in this overview of key themes, we should note that from the middle of the nineteenth century to the present, class analysis has been a common feature of Christian writing. One encounters arguments to the effect that God has special concern for the poor and the downtrodden, and occasional arguments that society requires a leisure class to preserve and cultivate the arts and the sciences. But more pronounced has been the resounding presumption that God favors the middle classes. "Classes," not "class," have been accented. Some stratification according to ability, effort, level of responsibility, and value to the community has been regularly presupposed. If people are poor and suffering, something is wrong either with them or with the social system that oppresses them. Something has to change so that they can become a part of the rather broadly construed middle classes. Sometimes this means personal conversion or reform, sometimes it means sustained and sacrificial charity, and sometimes it means social transformation and reform. To be sure, the nineteenth- and early twentieth-century thinkers would have agreed with the contemporary slogan of liberation theology — "God is on the side of the oppressed" — but they would have agreed because they also presupposed that everyone should be enabled to join the middle classes. Some (although not many) of these earlier thinkers also believed that some of the poor were in fact poor because of moral deficiency, of which a chief symbol during this period was the use of "demon rum." But even the struggle against such "moral defects" as alcoholism among working-class people soon took on the character of a crusade against the liquor merchants who exploited the poor. Prohibition was the eventual result.

Similarly, if people are so rich that they are no longer subject to the vicissitudes of life that daily affect their neighbors, if they are isolated from the needs of common humanity, and if they utilize their wealth to distort the structures of the common life for private ends, something is wrong either with them or with the structure of the social system that allows such uncontrolled special privilege. Certain authors articulated this presumption in works that were much less critiques of capitalism than sharp moral critiques of capitalists. Some capitalists might be converted and pursuaded to alter their behaviors, these authors believed, although in most situations the attempts to constrain crude greed also demanded systemic change. This critical attitude worked itself out in trust-busting, regulatory agencies, and progressive income-tax structures.

The original thinking in this area was done largely by "learned clergy." What they produced was the "social democratic" movements of the Continent, the Christian socialism of England, and the Social Gospel movements of the United States and Canada. The categories they constructed in the attempts to democratize economic life dominated large portions of Christian teaching and preaching. Indeed, the patterns of thought they formed became the core assumptions of "Christian social ethics" for most of the century, and gradually penetrated the convictions of the majority of Westerners. From that foundation, the chief principles for which they argued were institutionalized in public policy, although seldom with overt reference to their theological roots. Modern, Western political economies have not had a "pure" capitalism since, and it is incorrect to call any system influenced by such developments "capitalistic" without qualification. In the next chapter we will see some key examples of these developments.

Study Questions

This chapter discusses the tenth key theme of a Christian public theology: Christology. It traces a major extension of the classical doctrines of Christology in an effort to show the pertinence of Christ to modern political and economic structures.

1. The modern social sciences have modified many understandings of Scripture, Reason, and Experience. Do you think that contemporary theology should attend to these new understandings?

2. What is slavery? Why is the battle over slavery so important to our understanding of the Word in relationship to the world?

3. Define "pietism." Does it advance or retard Christian thought about the relationship of Jesus to social problems?

4. What are some examples of practices and beliefs which, although they are recorded in Scripture and have been a part of Christian

traditions for centuries, are no longer to be practiced because of belief in Jesus Christ as both divine and human?

5. Should Christians try to change public policy on the basis of their beliefs? If Christians base their public actions on an understanding of the life, teachings, and hope of Christ, why should non-Christians pay any attention?

6. Does "Christian sociology" really represent a new alliance of faith and a secular philosophy? What are some examples of "unholy alliances" of secular thought and Christianity? Are there also "holy alliances"? How can we tell the difference?

7. There are many teachings about economic matters in Scripture. Do the teachings of Jesus lead us to choose one form of economic structure over another?

8. Modern industrialization created new tensions between workers and managers and between the unemployed and the very rich. What attitude should we have toward these groups? What did Jesus mean when he said, "The poor you will always have with you"?

9. How is culture transformed by Christ? How do changing cultural patterns demand rethinking our Christology?

10. One of the values most celebrated by Americans is "respect for the individual." Is there any difference between that and "individualism" in politics and economics? Does our theological view of the individual differ from "individualism"?

11. Americans very often express great appreciation for "community life." Is there any difference between that and "collectivism" in economics and politics? Does a theological view of society differ from other views of collective life?

12. Classic Christian doctrine speaks of Christ as being of "two natures"—fully God and fully human. Do you think that has any practical implications for the ways in which individuals are and should be related to community?

13. Do you think that "Christian sociology" as it has developed in the last century is faithful to Scripture, responsible to Reason, in accord with Experience, and a genuine extension of Tradition? Why or why not?

CHAPTER FOUR

The Democratization of the Economic Order

Thus far we have identified the need for a public theology of political economy if we are to develop a vision of stewardship for modern life. We have also set forth the decisive touchstones of authority by which one might be developed, outlined some of the indispensable themes of a public theology, and shown how Christians began to develop a modern theology of economic life in the midst of rapid modernization and industrialization during the last half of the nineteenth century.

By the early twentieth century, the main options had been developed into a discernable spectrum of opinions under the general heading of "Christian sociology." Decisive in this way of thinking is the interpretation of the New Testament, and most especially the meaning of Jesus Christ for economic life. To illustrate both the major accents in this area and the poles of the spectrum, I will examine two books that summarize the work of the preceding several decades: Shailer Mathews's *The Social Teaching of Jesus* and Walter Rauschenbusch's *Christianity and the Social Crisis.*[1] The former is more "personalist" in focus; the second is more "communalist" in focus.

We should note that neither effort allows economic theory,

---

1. Mathews, *The Social Teaching of Jesus: An Essay in Christian Sociology* (New York: Macmillan, 1897); and Rauschenbusch, *Christianity and the Social Crisis* (New York: Macmillan, 1907). Subsequent references to these books will be made parenthetically in the text.

capitalist or socialist, to be unqualified. In their pure forms, these theories are simply inadequate to describe what is or to prescribe what ought to be the state of affairs in any modern political economy. Economic systems never work in a vacuum; they always function in a social context. And the most remarkable public theological consensus of modernity — exemplified by Mathews and Rauschenbusch and, indeed, shaped by movements they represent — is that social relationships ought to be "democratic." The term, originally a political one, is now applied to social and economic institutions and attitudes.

But what precisely is it that gives democracy in politics or economics its inner validity, its moral coherence, its spiritual fiber? Mathews and Rauschenbusch believe that the answer is to be found in Jesus Christ. A "scientific," fully historical, and fully rational "social exegesis" of the New Testament, with special reference to the life and teachings of Jesus, can provide us with a "Christian sociology," the capstone of a wide range of indispensable themes of a public theology for modern political economies. (The biblical passages that these two authors cite will be given in {}.)

SHAILER MATHEWS AND CHRISTIAN PERSONALISM

Mathews begins his book with an analysis of "Christian sociology." He makes it is quite clear that there is no Christian method of sociological investigation, and that the process of investigating social forces and results "can no more have an ethical — still less religious — character than the study of a crystal" (pp. 1-2). But whenever a scientific investigator attempts to formulate the results of investigation and to speak of the significance of what is found, ethics and religiously conditioned orientations are inevitable. Thus, in the same sense that we can speak of Aristotelian science or Baconian science (since both Aristotle and Bacon went beyond mere observation and generalized about the significance of what they found), we can speak of "Christian sociology." The particular bits of information are arranged in a particular way to offer a fuller interpretation of what is at stake in the information.

It is manifestly clear, Mathews argues, that Jesus did not provide systematized social teachings any more than he provided a systematic theology. Nevertheless, just as a skilled geologist working from general geological principles can infer certain deep structures of the earth by carefully examining certain outcroppings, so Christian sociology, working from the general principles of hu-

manity, can interpret social outcroppings as a form of socially related moral and spiritual being. Mathews asserts that Jesus Christ
taught the latter more acutely than even Plato, Aquinas, Kant, or
Hegel; and, indeed, Jesus' teaching has had more impact on the
world. To ignore this is simply intellectual dishonesty. At the same
time, some views of what Jesus taught have been wildly distorted,
and these distortions have also had an impact on the world—of a
quite negative sort.

"Christian sociology," as Mathews sees it, corrects previous
errors because it recognizes that anthropology is the clue to sociology. The Christian understanding of human nature is first of all
person-centered, with two distinct accents. First, the gospel presumes that to be human is to be *both* "body *and* soul, flesh *and*
spirit. . . . Jesus does not . . . regard the body as necessarily evil
{Matt. 10:28; Mark 10:8; 12:25; John 6:51-53}" (p. 23). Second,
this "physio-psychological being" is capable of merging "its life with
that of similar beings—that is, [it has a] capacity for social life. . . .
[Yet] sociability does not mean the extinction of individuality. . . .
There are attracting and correlating powers of the personality that
reach out to others and form . . . a new substance that is essentially
a unity derived through union. To disregard the promptings and
needs of this social part of the personality is to invite an intellectual
and moral death whose earliest symptoms are sin and abnormality
of all sorts" (pp. 27-28).

To secure this view of material and spiritual personhood in
"a unity of fellowship" as the basis for Christian social teachings,
Mathews explores the biblical images of the vine and the branches,
the mansion and its rooms, and the companionship of being yoke-
fellows {Matt. 11:27-30; John 15:1-2, 17:23}. "So great and essential" is this relational understanding of human nature that "the
whole significance of Jesus as a mere ethical teacher is overtopped
by it" (p. 31).

On this basis it is possible to see the ethical core of society
in a deeper sense. It has to do with actualizing a union that pre-
serves and enhances the person—just as membership in a healthy,
closeknit family does not inhibit but cultivates each member while
recognizing the sometimes sharp differences between each in ability, need, authority, and capacity to contribute to the whole. This
union, given distinctly ethical articulation in the term "Kingdom of
God," provides the model of the "ideal society." It is sometimes
experienced in life, and it is the basis of the quest for a new social
order.

Mathews argues that there are two common misuses and misunderstandings of such terms as "the Kingdom of God." One is the apocalyptic view in which a catastrophic end of the world is expected, when only the few elect will be rapturously and immediately taken into heaven. Mathews acknowledges that there are moments of almost fatalistic urgency in the New Testament, but he does not find the foreboding attitude toward the future that this view demands. In response to this lopsided perspective, he points to those passages where the Kingdom is seen as already among the people {Luke 17:20-21}, where the analogy is drawn to the growth of the seed in the field {Matt. 13:24-43}, where some have to struggle mightily in order to gain entrance {Matt. 11:12-15}, and where the Kingdom produces different results among different people {Mark 4:3-4}.

A second misuse of the Kingdom, Mathews says, is to offer it as a warrant for violent revolution in which militant parties attempt to seize power in order to establish a fully righteous political-economic order. Political enthusiasts of all ages have thus misunderstood the image, he points out, and he counters with several biblical examples: "[Jesus] refuses the tempting suggestion to become a new Caesar {Matt. 4:8-10}; later his disciples are warned against 'the leaven of Herod' — that is, of an overweening political ambition {Mark 8:15}; he flees from those who would force him into politics {John 6:15}" (p. 45). Instead, the Kingdom has to do with the moral vision of a loving, sharing, *social* order, initiated by God, centered in the community of faith. It is to be carried out in a life of freely chosen moral commitment by anyone who would become a brother or a sister of Christ. The reconstruction of the inner fabric of human relationships — and neither their apocalyptic abolition nor their forced realization by violent coercion — is what the New Testament is all about.

On this basis, Mathews offers an interpretation of the decisive areas of the common life in which Christians are to make concrete the vision given to them. For him the monogamous family is the obvious starting point. It is to be based on the "unitive sharing" and equality of the sexes, although these can take several different forms in particular lives. In Mathews's view, neither Scripture nor ethics based on it offers blueprints for institutions. But each does define basic boundaries within which humans must work out practical possibilities under specific conditions, and basic principles that are to guide decisions.

Similarly, a second area of life — politics — has to be discussed in terms of basic boundaries and basic principles. To say more betrays the text. In politics, according to current usage, Jesus cannot clearly be called a socialist, a monarchist, a republican, or a democrat. It is particularly inaccurate to call him a democrat if by the term we mean to suggest the advocacy of majority rule. All we can surmise is that the community of faith is not to become identical with the coercive structures of government and that both anarchy and tyranny are wrong. All political systems are to be evaluated by their capacities to avoid these perils and to sustain all persons in community. Constitutional democracy may do this best in our kind of world, but support for it cannot be read directly from the New Testament or the life of Jesus.

Mathews treats the decisive third area, economics, in a comparable way. He recognizes that in many aspects the New Testament can be easily misunderstood. Jesus is portrayed as speaking out harshly against the wealthy. In the saying about the camel and the needle's eye {Matt. 19:24}, in the parable about the beggar Lazarus and the rich man {Luke 16:19-31}, and in Jesus' delineation of the Christian life {Luke 12:33}, "it would seem as if the renunciation of wealth was one of the conditions of joining the new society."

> It would not be at all strange, therefore, if from these teachings and facts men should have concluded that the pursuit of wealth was unchristian and wealth itself an evil rather than a good. And so men have thought in all times since the days of Jesus. The preaching of the church against wealth has been equalled only by its zeal to obtain it. . . . [Nevertheless,] through the centuries in which the leaven of Jesus has been working in society, wealth has enormously increased. . . . The poor have been always present, and the Christian church has always endeavored, with more or less wisdom, to do them good. (Pp. 137-39)

In Mathews's view, a more balanced reading of the Scripture reveals that Jesus' critique of wealth is fundamentally about "his recognition of the relativity of goods" (p. 143). More important than material wealth is making our lives a part of others' lives. Thus the issue is not wealth itself but whether or not wealth is used for the establishment of genuine personhood and loving relationships. According to Mathews, "This is the only possible interpretation which can be placed upon that otherwise extraordinary parable of the unjust steward {Luke 16:1-13}" (p. 144). The questions Jesus poses to us are not "Are you wealthy?" or "Are you poor?" The questions are "What shall it profit a man if he gain the whole world and yet lose himself?" {Luke 9:25} and "Have you done the will of my father?" The point is that we cannot serve two masters. The struggle for fortune more often than not breaks down that sense of dependence that binds person to person and people to God.

> In the same proportion as the semblance of independence increases is there danger that a man will forget that he is always an integral part of society and that he can be truly a man only as he is dependent upon God and in sympathy with his fellows. . . . This is the secret of Jesus' command to trust the Heavenly Father for clothes and food {Matt. 6:31-33}. These things are not evil, but if once regarded as the highest good, they will inevitably lead to a selfish competition for personal advantage at the cost of generous impulses and faith. (P. 146)

All this, Mathews says, brings Jesus close to the moral impulses that lie behind much modern talk of socialism:

> If wealth is not for purely individual enjoyment, but is to be used for the good of society . . . , it is not a long step to the belief that any form of private property is anti-fraternal and that society itself can best administer economic matters for the good of its members. Something like corroboration is given such an interpretation of Jesus' position by the fact that the company of his followers had a common purse {John 12:19; 13:6}, and that the members of the primitive Jerusalem church "had all things in common" {Acts 2:44-45; 4:32, 36, 37}. (Pp. 148-49)

But Mathews does not think that, in the final analysis, the case can be made that Jesus was a socialist. "It is futile to attempt to discover modern socialism in the words of Jesus. There is, it is true, nothing incompatible with such a system were it once proved to be the means best adapted to furthering the true spirit of brotherliness" (p. 151). But the same might be said for other systems under a variety of conditions.

Further, those who argue that Jesus identified completely with the poor, those who call for the abolition of all private property or press every social policy toward complete material equality — these people simply have not read the gospel carefully. It is true that "no man ever had a deeper sympathy with the poor and unfortunate," and that Jesus "felt profoundly the misery and injustice which spring from the irresponsible power of the wealthy" (p. 147). But "it is a mistake to think of early Christians as altogether from the poorest classes. They were from the well-to-do and even wealthy classes as well," Mathews points out (p. 147n.1).

If [Jesus] was homeless, the houses of the rich were continually at his service. If his head was sometimes wet with the dews of heaven, he knew also what it was to have poured upon him costly ointment. The rich man Zacchaeus was welcomed quite as heartily by him as his fellow-citizen the beggar Bartimaeus. . . . [And] when his friends saw fit to criticize a woman who had anointed him, on the ground that the cost of the ointment might much better have been given to the poor, Jesus rebukes them. (Pp. 147, 154)

Nor can the story of Ananias and Sapphira properly be taken as an endorsement of a socialism that entails social ownership of the means of production (though many have tried to interpret the story this way). Their fate was not sealed by their failure to share all their property, for others in good standing in the community clearly did not do so. The problem was "their lying to the effect that they had so done" (p. 153). In Mathews's opinion, this is a quite different matter from a call for absolute equality. It simply cannot be argued on biblical grounds that Jesus demands equality in material things. As the parable shows us {Matt. 25:4-30; Luke 19:12-27}, "there are men to whom one talent could be entrusted, and those to whom five and ten" could be entrusted (p. 172).

In summarizing his views, Mathews argues that the key point derived from "Christian sociology" as it understands the meaning of Jesus for economic life is this: all wealth is to be fraternally gained and used. That is the substance of stewardship and the clue to a Christian understanding of political economy. Wealth is, in this sense, "a public trust — a principle that is made no less true from the fact that its application to the various problems of any age must be left to the age itself" (pp. 155-56). The conditions of the motivations and dispositions and the quality of will and social affection are the core of Jesus' message. Nevertheless, he unsparingly denunciates those who become wealthy "at the expense of souls; who find in capital no incentive to further fraternity; who endeavor so to use wealth as to make themselves independent of social obligations and to grow fat with that which should be shared with society" (p. 157).

Shailer Mathews represents one persistent wing of Christian teaching about modern economics. In various forms it is the substance of Christian approaches to business ethics. It is less anti-capitalism than it is anti-greed. It is social in the sense that it recognizes that people require both material resources and one another to be whole. And it is political in the sense that it calls for nonideological approaches to civic responsibility. But most of all, it is social and religious in the specific senses that it centers on the building of community relationships in the prepolitical structures of life, and does so on the basis of Christian love.

WALTER RAUSCHENBUSCH AND CHRISTIAN PROPHECY

Our second example of "Christian sociology" is more self-consciously "prophetic." Walter Rauschenbusch represents the other end of the spectrum. Such a distinction may be made despite the fact that Mathews and Rauschenbusch regularly quote each other and that it is possible to read passages from either without being sure which one wrote them. But while Rauschenbusch's work has many accents that are also found in Mathews's work, he has another side, which I will stress here. The difference arises not only because Rauschenbusch summarized and echoed the more radical voices of the previous half century, but also because he explicitly connected his view of Jesus and economics with the message of the Old Testament prophets. Thus his use of the Bible differs from that of Mathews. "A comprehension of the essential purpose and spirit of the prophets," wrote Rauschenbusch, "is necessary for a comprehension of the purpose and spirit of Jesus and of genuine Christianity. In Jesus and the primitive Church the prophetic spirit rose from the dead. . . . The real meaning of his life and the real direction of his purposes can be understood only in that historical connection" (p. 3).

All "natural" religions tend to worship "powers" and try to get human life "in tune" with them by ritualistic actions. The preferred powers may be the powers of nature, the powers of fertility and sexual potency, or the powers that govern peoples by force or wealth. But the prophets — from Moses to Amos, Hosea, Isaiah, Jeremiah, and Micah — are all "heralds of the fundamental truth that religion and ethics are inseparable, and that ethical conduct is the supreme and sufficient religious act." The prophets do not worship powers or cultivate cultic precision; they bring the plumb line of godly justice to measure them. They seldom focus on the private morality of personal life, or even on the family: "the twin-evil against which the prophets launched the condemnation of Jehovah was injustice and oppression" (pp. 7-8).

This is also, argues Rauschenbusch, the central message of John the Baptist, the figure in the New Testament whereby the explicit link is made between the ancient prophetic tradition and Jesus. Indeed, "the Christian movement began with John the Baptist. All the Evangelists so understood it {Matt. 3; Mark 1; Luke 3; John 1}" (p. 49). "In joining hands with John, Jesus clasped hands with the entire succession of the prophets with whom he classed John. . . . [Thus Jesus] was not merely an initiator, but a consummator. . . . He embodied the prophetic stream of faith and hope" (pp. 53-54).

But whereas the prophets had spoken of and to the righteousness of Israel, Jesus did away with the nationalistic features of the prophetic tradition. His message extended the core of the prophetic message further than the prophets could have imagined. Indeed, it became "universal in scope, an affair of all humanity" (pp. 62, 85ff.).

It would be a serious mistake, argues Rauschenbusch frequently, to understand Jesus *simply* as a revolutionary reformer or a moral teacher or an heir of the prophets. He was, as all the church has confessed, the Son of God, the crucified and resurrected Lord, the Savior of souls, the Christ. But it is precisely as these that he made the visions of the prophets concrete and bore within him the germs of a new social and political order that the devotees of Christ have regularly and repeatedly attempted to avoid.

There are several reasons for this neglect, some quite understandable, some less so. For one, as Rauschenbusch points out, "the early Christians did not belong to the literary class with whom the impulse to record its doings on paper is more or less instinctive." Thus our records are incomplete. Moreover, given the Roman suspicion of any issues that appeared to be social or political, there was good cause for "not writing them down or publishing them freely" (p. 95). Also, "Paul expected an immediate spiritualization of the entire Cosmos" (p. 104), and his influence came to dominate those branches of the church that emerged triumphant in the Mediterranean. In addition, the apocalyptic hope for the immediate return of Christ led some away from interest in "worldly" matters. Yet even in the records we have there are elements that, properly seen, have direct implications for our understanding of Christian attitudes on economic questions.

The apocalypticism that we see at several points in the New Testament, for instance, clearly implies "the overthrow of the present world-powers" and the constant seeking for new possibilities by discerning the signs of the times (pp. 110ff.). Subsequently, Christians have not seen the revolutionary aspects of this dimension of the gospel clearly present in the New Testament because they have so often been allied by class background, inclination, and

training that they have focused only on the spiritual, the individualistic, and the otherworldly features of the New Testament witness. Even otherwise highly respected contemporary scholars, judges
Rauschenbusch, are subject to this charge. Supported by personal
or official alliances between ecclesiasticism and privilege, and cut
off from the masses, Christians down through history have repeatedly turned to speculative reflection, ascetical disengagement,
personalistic pietism, and ritualistic ceremonialism — the means by
which the social-ethical dimensions of Jesus' teachings have been
successfully obscured.

Nevertheless, "a volatile spirit has always . . . [been present
in] organized Christianity and aroused [the faithful] to love freedom
and justice and their fellow-men" (p. 150). It is endemic to the spirit
of Christ even where it is not fully conscious or where it is partially
repressed.

> Has it not lifted woman to equality and companionship with man,
> secured the sanctity and stability of marriage, changed parental
> despotism to parental service, and eliminated unnatural vice, the
> abandonment of children, blood revenge, and the robbery of the
> shipwrecked from the [formerly approved] customs of Christian
> nations? Has it not abolished slavery, mitigated war, covered all
> lands with a network of charities to uplift the poor and the fallen,
> fostered the institutions of education, aided the progress of civil
> liberty and social justice, and diffused a softening tenderness
> throughout human life? (P. 147)

Insofar as these benefits have become features of Western
civilization under the influence of Christianity, we can honor our
history. Yet it must be acknowledged that the positive effects of the
church in its social witness have been due less to the conscious
intentions of the organized church or its ecclesiastically preoccupied
official thinkers than to its indirect and diffuse influences. There
is something in the message and spirit of Jesus that cannot be
entirely subverted. And at present — when the earlier, privileged
alliances of magistrates and clergy have been broken, when modern
biblical studies bring us into closer contact with the person and
context of Jesus, and when the contemporary social sciences open
new doors to the analysis of society and its institutions — we have
the possibility of making the indirect and diffuse influences of the
New Testament direct and intentional in public life. That is the
task of Christian sociology and the church generally today.

When we do turn to the direct application of the teachings of
Jesus to contemporary social life, we cannot avoid seeing the fun-

damental discrepancies. The governing social aim of Jesus was the Kingdom of God. Rauschenbusch points out, as does Mathews, that this concept has been subject to numerous interpretations and misinterpretations. It clearly is not dependent on human force or divine catastrophe, but "after all this has been said, it still remain[s] a social hope." It is still "a collective conception" with political overtones (p. 65). And today it is a vision particularly marked by a transformed attitude toward economics.

Jesus taught that "ye cannot serve God and mammon." In making this statement, Rauschenbusch says, Jesus was not merely pointing out a danger to the soul. "In his desire to create a true human society he encountered riches as a prime divisive force in actual life." When Jesus confronted the rich young man and bade him get rid of his wealth, the advice was partly for the good of the young man's soul. "But Jesus immediately rises from this concrete case to the general assertion that it is hard for any rich man to enter the kingdom of God" (p. 75). It does no good to try to make the case that the real problem was that the young man *trusted* too much in wealth for his own spiritual good. That interpretation is warranted neither by the best textual evidence we have nor by a thorough reading of the whole corpus of Jesus' sayings about wealth. "It gives a touch of cheerful enjoyment to exegetical studies," Rauschenbusch notes, "to watch the athletic exercises of interpreters when they confront these sayings of Jesus about wealth. . . . There is a manifest solicitude to help the rich man through [the needle's eye]." But the clear meaning cannot be missed: "It is hard to get riches with justice, to keep them with equality, and to spend them with love" (pp. 77-78). The social and not merely the individual meanings cannot be avoided.

The parable of the steward in Luke 16 presents a similar case. This passage has "often been so allegorized and spiritualized that the application to the rich has almost evaporated" (p. 80). But when the Pharisees of all ages scoff at such teachings, they must confront the story of Dives and Lazarus. It is Jesus' reply to such scoffing. The story is not intended to give information about the future life; it is intended to make a point about the treatment of the brothers of Dives. It has to do with "the gulf that separates the social classes" (p. 84).

Rauschenbusch's view of the prophetic Christ clearly corre- lates with his view of the wealthy: he portrays Jesus as the explicit ally of the poor and working class. He was a man of the common people, and he never deserted their cause as so many others have done.

> He had worked as a carpenter for years, and there was nothing in his thinking to neutralize the sense of class solidarity which grows up under such circumstances. The common people heard him gladly because he said what was in their hearts. His triumphal entry into Jerusalem was a poor man's procession; the coats from their backs were his tapestry. . . . During the last days in Jerusalem he was constantly walking into the lion's cage. . . . It was the fear of the people which protected him while he bearded the powers that be. His midnight arrest, his hasty trial, the anxious efforts to work on the feelings of the crowd against him, were all a tribute to his standing with the common people. (P. 84)

Clearly, the intention of Jesus — indeed, the intention recognized by Mary before Jesus himself was teaching — was that through him God would "put down the proud and exalt them of low degree, . . . fill the hungry with good things and send the rich empty away" {Luke 1:52-53}. "The first would be last and the last would be first" {Mark 10:31}. The poor and the hungry and the sad were to be satisfied and comforted. The meek who had been shouldered aside by the ruthless would get their chance to inherit the earth, even if conflict and persecution would be inevitable {Matt. 5:1-12}.

In Rauschenbusch's treatment of Jesus in these and other passages, we can see aspects of Christian sociology that are not present to any striking degree in Mathews's work. Rauschenbusch saw class analysis as a useful tool in biblical exegesis, and he was more directly and explicitly convinced that Jesus issued rather distinct guidelines for social arrangements as well as a command to love. For him, all led toward a democratization of the economic order in a distinctly socialist direction.[2] He did not base his argument on the New Testament alone, however. We have already seen that he read the New Testament through the prophetic tradition of the Old Testament. He also read it through a perspective on what happened to Christianity in postbiblical periods. He believed that the spirit of Christ had, over the centuries, gradually and painfully brought about the relative socialization of the church, the family, the school, and the political order. In each of these areas of life, people give according to ability and take according to need. Equality and mutual solidarity are governing principles if not always reigning prac-

---

2. See especially his book *Christianizing the Social Order* (New York: Macmillan, 1912).

tices. Things are held in common and disposed of by democratic means. For these gains we are indebted to those who grasped and fought for the message of the prophetic Jesus in earlier ages.

However, Rauschenbusch argued, all these are now threatened with destruction by the old echoes of feudalism and the new autocracies of the capitalist corporations, now aided and abetted by "the bloody law of tooth and claw" present in competitive economic theory. The present distribution of wealth, income, influence, and power—together with the governing principles, values, and goals that legitimate the present economic order—is a direct affront to everything for which Christ lived, taught, and died.

PERSONS IN COMMUNITIES/COMMUNITIES OF PERSONS

The ideas of Mathews and Rauschenbusch represent a certain range of views that had been under discussion for half a dozen decades before they wrote the works examined here. Other notable figures occupied distinguished places in the spectrum. These figures believed that trust in Jesus and his teachings would reveal the clue to economic ethics, and that neither the institutionalized greed of modern commerce nor the modern "science" of utilitarian economics could grasp either the actual character of human nature or the ethical principles necessary for the reconstruction of the economic order in modernity. They worked to establish a biblically based "Christian sociology" that would lead to the democratization of the economic order and clarify some basic boundaries and principles that could guide public discussions of economic ethics.

They all believed that God intended and Jesus taught that people are to be, economically, "persons in community." They also believed that people in their horizontal relationships and the institutions of community with their inevitably conditioned and temporal patterns were to be seen and measured by the vertical and eternal plumb line of God's truth, justice, and love, known in Jesus Christ. Some authors put the focus on personalism, others on communitarianism; none doubted the transcendent point of reference. "Persons in community" meant living "under God's justice" and "toward God's Kingdom."

We might draw an analogy between this discussion and early church debates about how it is that Jesus Christ is both "fully God" and "fully human." The main point of the doctrine seems to have been that something essential about the nature of the Savior is lost if he is viewed as only one or the other, or if one aspect becomes merely an addendum to the other, or if the two aspects are thought to be simply the same. Nor can a third reality be posited that is neither divine nor human or that makes Christ distinct from either humanity or God.

The logic of "Christian sociology" as it speaks to modern political economies is a logic fully in accord with other principles of a public theology such as creation and liberation, vocation and covenant, sin and freedom, ecclesiology, and the pluralism and unity of the Trinity, but its center is a kind of "two natures" under-standing of humanity based on the "two natures" of Christ. Persons are to live in community, and communities are to support and en-hance personhood. Something essential about the nature of eco-nomic life, upon which the concrete existence of millions depends, is lost if either only private interest or only collective structure is regarded. Neither one can be seen as merely the implication of the other; neither, given free rein, necessarily leads to the other. And it is nonsense to posit some third way that has no place for either personalism or communitarianism.

The figures mentioned above, in dialogue with the best social theories available to them, articulated a doctrine of "persons in community" that attempted to establish decisive boundaries and principles for modern Christian thinking about economic life. These boundaries did not describe how to conduct every strategy or how to make every decision, and disagreement within the spectrum is likely to continue. Yet this doctrine indicates where and when so-ciety is likely to lurch too far in one direction or another. If private interest and individual economic calculation — even if guided by the most enlightened personal motivations — are accented rather than social harmony, economic chaos results. If the accent falls entirely on collective action and class solidarity, even given a profound struggle for a just community, the inevitable result is economic czarism. In either case, "the wages of sin is death."

One of the remarkable things about these developments is that they entail a social view of economics rather than an economic view of society. The social nature of the human self and the neces-sity of applying spiritual and moral principles to the structured tissues of social relationship in community are presupposed, *and are viewed as empirically and normatively prior to economic activ-ity.* If, therefore, any fundamental change is to be made in economic life, it must be made first of all in the formation of principled human relationships and in the transformation of the fabric of ordinary structures of community — families, schools, hospitals, professions, unions, businesses, and political parties — before it can be institutionalized in political economies. Further, the clue to the transformation of human relationships and community structures is found in religion — specifically that kind of religion that is ethical in root and branch, that lives by a vision of the core principles and purposes of God summarized in the phrase "the Kingdom of God." Personal knowledge of Jesus Christ has these public theological implications. And if someone claims to have been saved, redeemed, or sanctified by Christ without being grasped by these impulses, it is in God's hands whether to take the claim seriously in heaven. On earth, such claims can make no difference in public discourse or policy formation.

SPREADING THE SOCIAL GOSPEL

At the time that this doctrine was being developed, two parallel movements were also underway within the churches. These were to play a distinctive role in the enfleshing of this doctrine in modern social history. One of these was the Sunday school movement; the other was the missions movement.

The Sunday School Movement

Those who developed the doctrine of Christian sociology were deeply engaged in the life of the churches. Many were pastors, some were seminary professors, and all were committed to the propagation of this doctrine among the laity. They preached in local churches and wrote for Christian journals. Very quickly they seized upon the opportunity to use their influence in the Sunday school programs, which had developed for both youth and adults during the nineteenth century. They wanted to get their message to the people. They were less inclined to speak directly to the public authorities or to issue public proclamations than to trust that a convinced laity would, through Christian citizenship, bring about the desired transformation of economic life. "Not by power, nor by might, but by every word that proceeds out of the mouth of the Lord" (Zech. 4:6).

The new social doctrine of economic life was taken as the main subject matter of a nationwide program of adult literature. Several denominations utilized this material in somewhat different fashions, but there was little variation in content and format throughout the literature. Series Number 1 of the 1910 program, for instance, correlated the biblical texts chosen for nationwide study in adult Sunday school classes with commentaries on the socioeconomic conditions of modern life.[3] It suggested strategies for lay people to actualize Christ's way in their own world of work and political economy. The topics discussed read like a somewhat quaint version of what later became known as the New Deal and the agenda of ecumenical Protestants from 1908 to the present.[4]

The series began with an analysis of the scriptural basis for "the ethics of work." With multiple references to biblical texts, God is represented as a creative worker. Humans are required to work; Christ is a worker, and the apostles and Saint Paul are also. Work is enjoined for all Christians. This means that when some are rich enough not to have to work, when others are too lazy to work, and when some are willing to work but fall victim to unemployment, the principles of the Bible are violated. Nor can wage earning or industrial production be considered the only arenas of work. As the series pointed out, the wives of many working men and farmers are not wage earners, but they are hard workers nonetheless. Further, the series called for an increase in artistic and creative labor. Merely routine manual labor, especially that requiring long hours, stunts the human ability to follow Christ. In typical fashion, the series offered a number of discussion questions such as "Should the state provide every man the opportunity to work?" and "Should there be a leisure class and a working class?"

From this starting point regarding economic life, the series went on to consider child labor (which "the whole spirit of Christianity forbids") and the role of "women in industry." First, it cited biblical texts that call attention to the heroines of Scripture who in special circumstances rose to leadership. Then it argued that the modern industrial order is a special circumstance, for "with machinery the world's work is becoming less and less a matter of muscle and more and more a matter of brain. Under the new conditions, man's superior physical strength counts for nothing in many occupations, while the finer nervous organization of women . . . [provides] precisely the conditions of success."[5]

---

3. *Studies in the Gospel of the Kingdom,* ed. Josiah Strong (Astor Place, N.Y.: American Institute of Social Service, 1910).

4. See Paul Allen Carter, *The Decline and Revival of the Social Gospel* (Ithaca, N.Y.: Cornell University Press, 1954); and Paul Bock, *In Search of a Responsible World Society: The Social Teachings of the World Council of Churches* (Philadelphia: Westminster Press, 1974).

5. *Studies in the Gospel of the Kingdom,* pp. 4, 9.

After tracing the negative effects of unequal pay for women and the possible negative consequences for family life if the internal structure of family living were not reconstituted, the series turned to the general problem of wealth and capital. With copious references to biblical materials and to contemporary statistics regarding growing discrepancies between the classes, the series emphasized the social basis and hence the social obligation of all wealth. The series further called for political control over unconstrained corporatism, supported the development of trade unions, and suggested ways to implement health and safety standards in industry.

In a similar fashion, the series dealt with the problems of housing, public utilities, and civic corruption, and with socialism as a solution. On the domestic front, it also paid special attention to the race question, labor conditions, prison reform, and immigration policies; its discussion of foreign relations took up the problems of colonialism, international arbitration, and peace. Throughout these discussions the series made use of capitalist and socialist literature in economics, subject to the core doctrine that Mathews and Rauschenbusch had helped articulate.

The agenda is not new now, and it was not new then. Its pithiness reflects more than half a century of ad hoc writings and several decades of efforts at systematic statement. The principles it enunciated and the methods of study it used have dominated the agenda for much populist work in Christian social ethics to this day.

The Missions Movement

In ways paralleling the Sunday school movement, the mission societies were also developing. Although the early American mission societies were formed in the first decades of the nineteenth century, it was after various denominations formed women's boards of missions (during the period from 1868-71) that the movement grew most rapidly. In this organization too the new doctrine of "persons in community" became dominant. Although much of the missionary effort was driven by the evangelical impulse to convert individual souls to Christ, and although there were constant temptations to make the mission stations outposts for political and economic as well as cultural imperialism, it is clear that the missions movement tended to undercut hard-line divisions between denominations and to give the whole church a more cosmopolitan perspective. As Shailer

Mathews was to write in his autobiography in 1936, many involved in the missions movements

> never realized that evangelization was . . . one aspect of the inter-penetration of western and eastern cultures, but the psychology of a generation stirred to religious enthusiasm by the call to transform a world was changed. Within it there was no surreptitious impe-rialism. . . . What would have been the result if industrialism, mil-itarism and science had been the only forms of [international contact] . . . is not difficult to imagine. But thousands of young men and women . . . interpreted the ideals of the West to peoples who have known only exploitation.[6]

Among these ideals were the reforms implied in the doctrine of Christian sociology and "the Kingdom of God" as the dominant vision. Every place that the international mission movement developed saw the planting of schools, hospitals, organizations for the improvement of the status of women, drives for the recognition of human rights, and movements to establish democracy, as well as churches. More often than not, these efforts were in direct tension with the commercial and imperialist interest of colonial powers.[7]

The interest in missions prompted the development of a number of "homeland missions" as well. Numerous such societies had been formed soon after the Civil War to aid the newly freed blacks, and by the late nineteenth century nearly every major city had at least one City Missionary Society; many had several societies. To coordinate this work, Baptists, Presbyterians, Congregationalists, Methodists, and Disciples (sometimes with the cooperation of Epis-copalians and Lutherans) frequently got together to form inter-denominational committees. The advocates of Christian sociology saw in these constituencies a way of enfleshing a public theology that would transcend the artificial divisions of dogma that kept the Body of Christ apart. They also saw the cooperative work involved as a way of uniting the churches on social and economic problems.

The path from these early committees to a genuine ecumeni-calism is long, slow, and complex. But there is no doubt that the origins of the ecumenical movement in America are in the homeland

---

6. Mathews, *New Faith for Old* (New York: Macmillan, 1936), pp. 34-35.
7. See T. Christenson and W. R. Hutchison, *Missionary Ideologies in the Imperialist Era* (Copenhagen: Arhus, 1981); E. J. Dunn, *Missionary Theology: Foundations in Development* (Lanham, Md.: University Press of America, 1980); and Max L. Stackhouse et al., *Apologia: Contextualization, Globalization, and Mission in Theological Education,* forthcoming.

missionary societies of the late nineteenth century and that the Christian response to economic changes (on the bases sketched in this chapter) brought about the core agreements that made possible the formation of the Federal Council of Churches in 1908.

The Federal Council of Churches, consisting of thirty Protestant denominations, called its first major pronouncement "the Social Creed." It was slightly modified in 1912 and again in 1932, but it has remained basically unchanged since. It began by stressing the authority of the New Testament and of Jesus for dealing with economic and social matters: "The problems of modern industry can be interpreted and solved only by the teachings of the New Testament, and Jesus Christ is the final authority in the social as well as in the individual life." The statement continued by declaring that the church was confronted by "the most significant crisis . . . of its long career," and then proceeded to address the crisis by putting the Federal Council and its member churches on record as favoring a lengthy list of social reforms. Not all were economic. Some were political and some were not. Some were closer to the traditional themes of biblical social criticism than others. Among other things, the list proposed equal rights for all, the end of poverty, health conservation, an end to child labor, the establishment of women's rights in the workplace, safer working conditions, accident insurance and pensions for workers, shorter working hours and a living wage for all, unions and employer-employee bargaining to settle industrial disputes, and protection of the individual and society alike from liquor traffic. Ending the list was a call for "the application of Christian principles to the acquisition and use of property, and for the most equitable division of the product of industry that can be ultimately devised." The statement concluded with a declaration that took its key phrase directly from earlier Christian sociologists: "The final message is redemption, the redemption of the *individual* in the *world*. . . . There is no redemption of either without the redemption of the other."[8]

Within a decade, comparable statements had been ratified in official actions by the particular denominational bodies, and these statements became the official stances of mainstream Christianity. Robert Moats Miller has traced the actions of the Methodists, the Northern Baptists, the Presbyterian Church, the Congregationalists, the Episcopalians, the Disciples, the Reformed Church, the

---

8. See A. D. Ward, *The Social Creed of the Methodist Church: A Living Document* (Nashville: Abingdon Press, 1961), p. 317.

Evangelical Synod of North America, and the Unitarians.[9] All argued that property rights are not sacred when they lead to the violation of basic human rights. All shared the conviction that a just society required the substitution of a "cooperative commonwealth" for industrial autocracy, possessive individualism, and a competitive capitalism driven by greed.

It is not possible to trace accurately, within the confines of this chapter, the degree to which these religious voices determined the formation of the New Deal. What is clear is that when the pressures of the Depression of the 1930s struck America, it was the specific policies advocated by these church leaders that became the policies of the nation. This happened with very little reference to the religious character of the perspective on social issues as they had actually developed. Nevertheless, this situation gives us some clues about how public theological matters have concrete historical consequences. They seldom shape public policy directly; they do shape the public in such a way that when — often decades or generations later — crises strike and policy decisions have to be made, the public has woven into the fabric of the ethos certain senses of boundaries and governing principles that predispose it to embrace certain options and to reject others.

TODAY: CHRISTIAN SOCIOLOGY IN DECLINE

Contemporary religious leadership, especially at the pastoral level, seems ignorant of this tradition of Christian sociology. They are confused about what contribution, if any, Christian thinking has to make to economic life. The churches of which they are a part often pass resolutions in direct continuity with the earlier traditions, but clergy seldom pay much attention or know the source of these concerns. They confine their views of stewardship to fundraising, while members of their congregations take their cues for social and economic policies from the secular press, from political ideologies, or from the sheer calculation of personal, class, or corporate interest, without reference to either piety or theology.

There are several possible causes of this recent break in and current ignorance about the tradition. For one thing, the focus of religious thinking about public issues shifted, in the heat of the battle against Hitler and the cold war against Stalinism, from eco-

---

9. Miller, *American Protestantism and Social Issues: 1919-1939* (Chapel Hill, N.C.: University of North Carolina Press, 1958).

nomic questions to political ones. (As the adage puts it, "It's hard to concentrate when you're up to your knees in crocodiles.") At the same time, the institutionalization (in the New Deal) of much that had been advocated by the older tradition of economic reform predisposed those who had a persistent interest in economic questions to turn to political channels to accomplish their ends. So did the newer issues of "civil rights," prompted by the betrayal of promises made to ex-slaves, American involvement in Vietnam, and the international movements toward decolonialization and hopes for rapid development through governmental programs. Thus politics, expressed in a confidence in state policies to realize economic righteousness, began to dominate the concerns of those who would be the natural heirs of this tradition.

Second, the enormous growth of the influence of psychology began to displace some of the earlier emphasis on sociological issues in theological education. Pastoral care in the ecumenical churches and psychological techniques for conversion in the evangelical churches tended to become the definition of "applied Christianity" as the state assumed wider welfare functions. The religious substance and moral shape of social institutions became less and less interesting to many as theological matters were privatized and individualized.

In addition, new perspectives on biblical studies undercut the perceived reliability of turning to the New Testament for ethical guidance in public affairs. Under the impact of the Bultmannian revolution in historical studies of the Bible, "the principles of Jesus" seemed to evaporate in the hot winds of existential "decisionism," and the relevance of the gospel message to any social issue became more difficult to state. The discontinuity between the testimony of the early church and modern culture was accented to the degree that many wondered if there was much continuity between biblical materials and present modes of thinking. Only recently have post-Bultmannian scholars begun to think again about the social and ethical implications of the New Testament, and seldom are they familiar with the tradition of "Christian sociology."

Further, economics in practice and economics as a social science developed in geometric ratios of increasing complexity so that they seemed much less amenable to social, philosophical, ethical, and religious analysis. The skyscraping towers of industry and finance began to dwarf the steeples of the churches, and the heavily mathematical econometric models programmed into the computers did not seem to leave much space for the inclusion of social or religious variables.

Ecumenically and socially oriented ecclesiastical bodies drew on the intellectual capital that had been built up during the first three quarters of our elongated century to advocate an enormous agenda of action on particular social issues. However, these bodies rarely attempted to cultivate the body of scholarship or a "public theology" that could discerningly guide action. The rising influence of non-Protestant groups also made these efforts less compelling to those who did not share such approaches to Scripture. "Actionism," based on the mobilization of material interests, became a temptation to many "praxis-oriented" advocates of social change. Simultaneously, the fantastic growth of the secular university system disinclined scholars who were interested in economics from turning to any "Christian sources." Instead, economics became increasingly "the science of the American dream," cut off from overtly religious and normative ethical issues. Indeed, when figures such as John Kenneth Galbraith want to be particularly acerbic in destroying an opponent, they call their opponent's view "theological." Yet, ironically, "denominational sectarianism" and "confessionalism" seem to be more rampant among economic theorists than among religious groups.

In brief, our study of the use of biblical resources in contemporary reflection on ethics and economics will have to take place in the context of a century-long tradition, now in decline because of neglect, that involves a spectrum of beliefs about the core of Christ's teachings and a variety of non-laissez-faire and non-collectivist understandings of economic life, usually grouped under the term "Christian sociology."

To proceed any further in our explorations, we will have to reach out more ecumenically than we have thus far. We will have to focus on certain key theorists who articulated influential new views about how religion influences economics in social history. Further, we will have to survey several new developments in Catholic and neo-evangelical thought. This is what we will undertake in the following chapter.

Study Questions

This chapter examines the ideas of several modern advocates of "Christian sociology" who attempt to show that their views of Jesus, based on the record of his life in the New Testament, can and do give us guidance about how to live in a modern industrial society quite different from the world of the early church.

1. The Bible does not speak of modern systems like capitalism and socialism and democracy. Do you agree with the Christian sociologists who say that we can, nevertheless, use the New Testament in making judgments about these things?

2. The founders of "Christian sociology" all believed that democracy is the proper form of government, and that its appropriateness is implied by basic Christian principles. Do you agree? Can people in non-democratic countries also be Christians? Can people who actively oppose democracy be Christians?

3. These authors also believed that the great challenge of our age is to bring democracy to economic life. How do you understand "economic democracy"? If more people became Christians, would their countries become more democratic politically and economically?

4. Is missionary work sometimes the instrument of political and economic interests and ideologies? What are modern examples of conflict and tension between commercial/imperialist interests and the efforts of missionaries?

5. If "Christianization" implies, in some sense, "democratization," does the "democratization" of an economy imply either capitalism or socialism?

6. Can capitalists be Christians? Can socialists be Christians?

7. Does your understanding of Jesus make any difference in the way you evaluate economic philosophies and systems? In the way you conduct business?

8. Can Hindus, Muslims, Buddhists, and atheists come to the same views of economic life that Christians have?

9. Is there any danger in an economy that does not have a theological base? Would we be better off if we kept religion out of economic questions?

10. Do you think Shailer Mathews is correct in his assertion that the primary influence of Christianity comes through its capacity to shape individuals and interpersonal relationships?

11. Do you think Walter Rauschenbusch is correct in his assertion that Christianity is best understood as a prophetic social movement that all Christians are called to enhance?

12. Do you think there are important relationships between our economic life and other structures in society such as the family, the educational system, and the legal system? Does Christianity relate to some of these in ways it does not relate to other social structures?

13. Is the "family of faith" in the "household of God," where all are brothers and sisters, the best model for society? What would that mean for modern economic institutions such as unions and corporations?

14. The advocates of "Christian sociology" used Sunday school, adult study groups, and youth organizations to advance their ideas. Should contemporary leaders do the same?

15. With all the changes in society, do some things remain the same? Does human nature change? How would your view contribute to our understanding of the relationship of the teachings of Jesus to modern political economy?

CHAPTER FIVE

Ecumene and Economy

The early leaders of "Christian sociology" brought about a relative consensus among ecumenically oriented Protestants: the gospel of Jesus Christ demands that we become "persons in community," heeding our vocations in covenant with others under God's law and living toward the Kingdom. We must attend to the material as well as the spiritual dimensions of life, the social as well as the individual dynamics of existence. These accents became the new core of stewardship and the dominant themes of the emerging efforts to reconstruct a public theology. Yet for all its influence among ecumenical theologians, pastors, and church leaders, this vision remained a minority report in the larger picture of Christian thought. Most "theologies" remained confessional, denominational, and focused on individual and otherworldly or ecclesiastical matters. Still, what we have seen in particular form in the United States had parallels in Great Britain, in many Commonwealth nations, and on the Continent.[1] Intentional action to incarnate this doctrine in societal practice, it was believed, would defeat the pathologies of laissez-faire capitalism, avoid the tyrannies of nationalistic or Bolshevik collectivism, and bring about the democratization of the economic order in modern political economies. This consensus held sway among the leadership in ecumenically oriented Protestant churches for more than half a century, sometimes taking a more

---

1. See R. Preston, *Church and Society in the Late Twentieth Century: The Economic and Political Task* (London: SCM Press, 1983).

democratic socialist direction, and at other times taking a more democratic capitalist direction.[2]

On the whole, these patterns of thought and action remained essentially Western. Only occasionally did they become central to the new churches founded by the missions movements of the nineteenth century and early twentieth century. Nevertheless, the growing world ecumenical movement, as well as the crises of two world wars, had begun to globalize the perspective of the churches and raise questions about the pertinence of such ideas to non-Western contexts.

But around the world such notions stood in tension with traditional Christian evangelism as well as with both traditional cultures and new, powerful political-economic visions that sought to bring social change on nontheological bases, ones that did not require conversion to Christ or that explicitly repudiated the notion that Jesus Christ had anything to do with the political and economic problems of the day. The ideas of Karl Marx, which had seemed to come to naught by the early failure of the Communist International, became a living, world-historical reality when Lenin put them into practice in 1917 and began an earthshaking experiment in "scientific socialism." And, a generation later, in a militantly romantic reaction against both liberal capitalism and Marxist socialism, Hitler erected a new form of "national socialism." Such developments made it clear that the problems of political economy could no longer be thought about in terms of national policies alone. Both politically, in the form of military power, and economically, in the application of "rational" technological means to production and distribution, the questions of political economy were global in scope and seemed to have less and less to do with specifically Christian theology.

SOME HISTORICAL ECUMENICAL STATEMENTS

The awareness of the international character of the "industrialization" of the world — often called "rationalization" at that time — coincided with the growing recognition of the international and transdenominational character of the world church. The mission churches of the nineteenth century were developing their own perspectives. They were raising questions about the omniscient pre-

---

2. See R. M. Miller, *American Protestantism and Social Issues: 1919-1939* (Chapel Hill, N.C.: University of North Carolina Press, 1958).

tenses of their parent churches. The silliness of sectarian divisiveness that plagued Protestantism was also recognized as a peril that prevented any unified Christian voice on precisely those political and economic issues that now engulfed colonialized or (later) decolonializing and developing nations. The quest for a more adequate ecumenical definition of a public theology as it related to the crises of modern political economies was subsequently intensified by the Depression.

In August of 1925, Christians shaped by several factors — the deeper tradition of "Christian sociology," the missions movements, and the awareness of the need to reassert and clarify a Christian understanding of social ethics in the face of these global developments — gathered in Stockholm at the Universal Christian Conference on Life and Work. There they confessed their sins of Christian omission and commission in social, economic, and political matters. They attempted to deepen and purify their devotion to the One they called "the Captain of our Salvation":

> Responding to His call "Follow Me,' . . . [they] accepted the urgent duty of applying His Gospel in all realms of human life — industrial, social, political and international. [They also declared that] the soul is the supreme value, that it must not be subordinated to the rights of property or to the mechanism of industry; . . . that industry should not be based . . . on the desire for individual profit, but that it should be conducted for the service of the community. Property should be regarded as stewardship for which an account must be given to God. Co-operation between capital and labour should take the place of conflict, so that employers and employed alike may be enabled to regard their part in industry as the fulfillment of a vocation.[3]

Further, in regard to social issues such as inadequate housing, unemployment, education, family life, and the exploitation of women and children, they argued that individualistic attempts at solution are inadequate: "The community must accept responsibility for them, and must exercise such social control over individual action as in each instance may be necessary for the common good. . . . [In such areas] the Church must contend not for the rights of the individual as such, but for the rights of the moral personality."[4]

In their efforts they seemed to recognize that previously they

---

3. World Council of Churches, "Stockholm: Official Report," in *Ecumenical Documents on Church and Society* (Geneva: WCC Press, 1954), p. 3.

4. "Stockholm: Official Report," p. 4.

had not adequately addressed the people on the lower fringes of life on whom the burdens of crisis fell most heavily. They thus addressed the young people of all countries, calling them to the "service of the Kingdom of God and of humanity." And they addressed the "workers of the world": "In the name of the Son of Man, the Carpenter of Nazareth we . . . deplore the causes of estrangement between the churches and the worker's movements, and express solidarity with the worker's aspirations after a just and fraternal social order."[5]

Three years after this Stockholm conference, the next step in international social witness was taken by the growing ecumenical movement. Meeting in Jerusalem, it brought together the various missionary societies and made Christianity and industrialism a major focus. The statement they made is more focused on the "community" side than on the "person" side of the formula: "The Gospel of Christ contains a message, not only for the individual soul, but for the world of social organization and economic relations in which individuals live. . . . When He wept over Jerusalem, He lamented the spiritual ruin, not merely of an individual, but of a whole society."[6] They affirmed the "sanctity of personality," but we can also note a new emphasis on "corporate responsibility." They drew the model for industrial corporations from the very nature of the church in a way that the American Social Gospel never spelled out. They understood the Christian church as a "society," a "body," and a "fellowship" that embraces

> all human relationships in which all are members one of another. . . . All forces therefore which destroy fellowship — war, economic oppression, the selfish pursuit of profits, the neglect of the immature, the aged, the sick or the weak — are definitely and necessarily in sharp contradiction with the spirit of Christianity. . . . [On this basis] it is the duty [of the church] to speak and work fearlessly against social and economic injustice . . . , to lend its support to all forces which bring nearer the establishment of Christ's Kingdom in the world of social relations, of industrial organization, and of economic life.[7]

The conference participants took up a series of questions that had to do with the ways in which "modernization" impacts coun-

---

5. "Stockholm: Official Report," p. 5.
6. "Jerusalem: Official Report," in *Ecumenical Documents on Church and Society,* p. 7.
7. "Jerusalem: Official Report," pp. 5, 7.

tries previously unaffected by it. I summarize four of the main elements in the rather lengthy and carefully worded statement they issued:

• Investments of capital and the development of natural resources in undeveloped areas must take place on terms that contribute to the welfare of indigenous peoples.
• Loans to undeveloped areas should be subject to international political controls.
• Private investments should not in any case carry rights to political control.
• "Contract labor" pay rates, working and living conditions, and restrictions on worker's freedoms must be carefully controlled.[8]

Within a year of this conference at Jerusalem, the "crash" that inaugurated the Depression struck. Once again the ecumenical groups gathered, this time in London. Drawing on the previous conferences, they focused on Christian sociology, "unemployment" (especially as found in those countries trying to follow the economic policies of Adam Smith), international labor movements (especially as they were turning to Marxism), and the "rationalization" of modern economic institutions. The conference asserted that "the present social order — in which is included a particular economic and financial policy — stands condemned as godless and as militating against true progress. . . . Viewed in the light of Natural Law and, supremely, of the Law of God in Christ . . . any system which runs contrary to the will of God is ultimately self-destructive, for only that which conforms to His will can be rational and can contain enduring life."[9]

Regarding unemployment, those gathered identified a fundamental flaw in the dominant economic doctrine of capitalism: it had not yet demonstrated that it could overcome inequities of distribution or the anguish of workers displaced by its cycles. These problems were practically and morally severe both within industrialized societies and between nations. In response, the reports from this conference called for the development of international conventions on the working, housing, medical, safety, and wage conditions of the laboring classes. This response acknowledged the Marxist claim that the dominant political and economic institutions

---

8. "Jerusalem: Official Report," pp. 11-17.
9. "London Conference Report," in *Ecumenical Documents on Church and Society*, p. 23.

were not adequately geared to the just support and protection of the working classes. At the same time, however, it resisted solutions that would further polarize the classes or that would deny the pertinence of Christian principles to questions of economic organization or policy.

In the "rationalization" of modern life the conferees saw "the signature of the trend of development in intellectual and social problems." Unconstrained, it aggravated the specific problems of modern industry, particularly as it gave "added momentum to a tendency seemingly natural with the whole of the modern world, viz., to organize itself on a completely un-Christian basis." Thus they called for the establishment of new contacts with "responsible groups in industry" and with labor to find out the degree to which "personal responsibility can have any play in a more and more depersonalized system of industry." Of special interest were the growth of monopoly, the power of trusts, and an "industrial patriarchalism," which are viewed as anomalies of the present age.[10]

Comparable themes to those mentioned so far were taken up in Basel in 1932 and in Geneva that same year. A year later, still another conference — this one at Rengsdorf — reached an agreement that can serve as a summary of what were to date the major themes of the growing economical consensus. Among the major themes were these:

- Work is a duty of every adult.
- Property is a loan, entrusted by God, for which a stewardly account has to be given. Property rights are not absolute.
- Economic activity is to be seen as a service to our fellows and to the community at large.
- Economic life must be subject to the demands of justice; it is not a sphere autonomous from ethics.
- Political authority is ordained by God, but God does not prescribe any particular form of the state, so long as the state is "limited.' Democracy, in its several possible forms, seems to limit state power under modern conditions.
- Political authority must keep to its proper sphere, and must not violate the rights of the individual, other associations in society, the family, or the Church.[11]

---

10. "London Conference Report," p. 28.

11. "Rengsdorf Statement," in *Ecumenical Documents on Church and Society,* pp. 44-47.

The introduction of these explicit formulations about political life in conjunction with economic life reflects the growing awareness that in both Fascist and Communist lands, the line between these two spheres of human activity was being intentionally obliterated. At the same time, the conference participants seemed to approve of steps toward "Laborite" democratic socialism in England and increased political intervention in some aspects of economic life by New Deal forms of democratic capitalism in America.

The greatest of these pre–World War II conferences was held in Oxford in 1937. The eight volumes that came out of these deliberations represent perhaps the most profound concerted work on social and economic questions by the greatest theological minds the Western world has produced in the twentieth century.[12] In the midst of the impending struggle against Fascism, they articulated most of the themes treated thus far in this chapter. The gifted minds and pens of J. H. Oldham, Emil Brunner, F. W. Farrar, C. H. Dodd, Christopher Dawson, Paul Tillich, William Temple, Reinhold Niebuhr, Kenneth Scott Latourette, and many more fill these pages with historical depth, theological insight, and contextual analysis that has seldom been matched. These figures effected the culmination of the strides made earlier and transmitted a tradition, cast in new keys, that during and after World War II was to dominate theological and ethical thought in America and, to some extent, around the world. They condemned in vibrant language laissez-faire capitalism, Soviet Communism, and "fascistic National Socialism." The dominant forms of twentieth-century political economies were all morally and spiritually corrupt and did not have the internal resources to reconstruct themselves.

In view of such wickedness, they argued, Christians might sometimes have to use force to restore justice when any of these systems became too powerful. Ideas of some "natural" evolution to benevolent systems and of pacifist hopes for totally nonviolent reconstruction were repudiated. The foundations were laid for Christian participation in the violent struggle against the most vicious of the three modern political economies — national socialism — and

---

12. See *The Oxford Conference Books*, 8 vols., ed. J. H. Oldham et al. (London: Willett Clark, 1938). For important treatments of subsequent developments, see Paul Bock, *In Search of a Responsible World Society: The Social Teachings of the World Council of Churches* (Philadelphia: Westminster Press, 1974); and *Faith and Science in an Unjust World*, 2 vols., vol. 1: *Plenary Presentations*, ed. Roger Shinn; vol. 2: *Reports and Recommendations*, ed. Paul Abrecht (Geneva: WCC Press, 1980).

for the necessity of using power to reconstruct societies beset by the pathologies of unconstrained capitalism and Communism. On these bases World War II was fought, and with these themes in mind the post-World War II conference in Amsterdam was able to address a sobered and broken world with a call for a new vision of "the responsible society."

In these developments we can see two major shifts away from "Christian sociology" as it had developed earlier. At the level of social analysis, "power" required a more subtle understanding than the leaders of the Social Gospel had given it. And, at the theological level, less and less reference was made to "the teachings of Jesus." Greater emphasis fell on both theological themes of the Christian faith and "natural law" theories of justice. This shift reflects a turning away from the more "evangelical" modes of exegesis of the earlier decades and a moving toward a more "catholic" mode of thought. It also is evidence of a certain resistance to the influence of Kierkegaard, who was newly discovered in this period, and, indeed, to Karl Barth, whose influence was growing in a number of theological centers. Whatever contributions these figures have made, the existential theology of the one and the dogmatic "confessional" theology of the other seemed unable to offer guidance on public issues of political economy.[13]

In addition, we must note two widely acknowledged limitations of these conferences. First, voices from the "Third World" were few and far between. The Tambaram Conference held in Madras in 1938 only partially remedied this situation. As the mission churches of Asia, Africa, and South America began to develop more independence from their mother churches in the West, especially in the aftermath of the decolonialization brought on by World War II, they began to face the problems of development and exploitation of their new countries by two forces: the residues of colonial power, and the new domestic elites, who were fascinated either by the Soviet Union's leap from a backward nation to a world power by centralized planning, or by new forms of romantic nationalism, which also placed economic control in the hands of a political-technocratic leadership. These "newer churches" of the Third World, freed from colonial political domination but still in various stages of economic "underdevelopment" or direct dependency, were to introduce a new urgency into the debates about economic systems,

---

13. See Robin Lovin, *Christian Faith and Public Choices: The Social Ethics of Barth, Brunner, and Bonhoeffer* (Philadelphia: Fortress Press, 1984).

particularly those aspects of modernization and rationalization that began to shatter traditional economies — indeed, whole cultures. The quest for a "third way" between Communism and capitalism became pervasive. To this day, post–World War II theories are strewn with the litter of "African socialism," "Asian socialism," and "Latin American socialism," all of which attempted to use political means to enforce modernizing economic development while "preserving" the values of the indigenous, traditional cultures. Much of contemporary liberation theology echoes these developments and their failures.

The conferences were also limited because conversations with Roman Catholic Christians over the questions raised by the conferences were very restricted. The "social encyclicals" from the 1890s through the Second World War were laying a groundwork for a less Roman and a more Catholic theory that was to reach genuine ecumenicity only with Vatican II. In Europe, the "worker priests" were reviving a populist, labor-oriented mode of ministry which spiritually echoed that of Saint Francis. Frequently they replaced the classical philosophies of Plato and Aristotle, used in previous Roman Catholic social thought, with the modern theories of Rousseau and Marx. These came to dominate a number of missionary orders and became supportive of the "third way" sought by developing nations. And in America, individual voices (from Monsignor John K. Ryan to Father John Courtney Murray) and official ecclesiastical statements such as "The Bishops' Program of Social Reconstruction" of 1919 and "The Church and the Social Order" of 1940 were developing modes of thought that eventually were to converge toward issues that all Christians now face.[14]

SOME HISTORICAL SOCIOECONOMIC THEORIES

While these developments were taking place in the formation of a new "ecumene" on the Christian side of "Christian sociology," another major development was underway in "economics" on the sociology side. It involves a mode of thought that is not widely understood among modern theologians and church leaders. And yet, this new social interpretation of political and economic life may provide a way of thinking about the relationship between theolog-

---

14. See B. L. Masse, *The Church and Social Progress* (St. Paul, Minn.: Bruce Publishing, 1966); and *The Faith That Does Justice*, ed. J. C. Haughey (New York: Paulist Press, 1977).

ical matters and social matters that avoids the common pitfalls of
individualistic and collectivistic theories.

Max Weber published his essay *The Protestant Ethic and the
Spirit of Capitalism* in two volumes of a German scholarly journal
in 1903-1904. The essay was the subject of much critical comment
on the Continent, and within a few years Weber issued a new
edition that responded to these criticisms. He later wrote three volumes on religion and economics in comparative cultures as well as
a massive systematic work, *Economy and Society,* with extensive
treatment of the social importance of religion as a factor shaping historical developments.[15] Weber's colleague, Ernst Troeltsch,
adopted aspects of Weber's thought and included them in his massive *Social Teaching of the Christian Churches.*[16] And later, R. H.
Tawney, the noted British Labourite scholar, gave his famous lectures (published as *Religion and the Rise of Capitalism),*[17] which
took Weber's earlier essay as their point of departure. In them
Tawney fundamentally distorted portions of Weber's argument and
offered a "counterargument" under the guise of a "supplementary"
argument, but he opened the whole discussion of Weber's ideas to
English-speaking audiences. Within a decade, a significant shift
had begun in the economic thinking of the leading Protestant scholars of the West.

Although a number of widely regarded theologians continue
to misinterpret what is at stake in these debates,[18] a transition has
taken place. To put the matter briefly, no longer can theologians
and religious ethicists take Adam Smith and Karl Marx to be the
chief "scientific" voices in regard to the nature and character of
capitalism. Both of these men held that economic structure, development, and process were not — and ought not to be — governed by
religious considerations, and for half a century ecumenical thinkers

---

15. See his *Protestant Ethic and the Spirit of Capitalism* (New York: Scribner's, 1958), and *Economy and Society: An Outline of Interpretive Sociology,*
3 vols., ed. G. Roth and C. Wittich, trans. E. Fischoff et al. (Totowa, N.J.: Bedminster Press, 1968). See notes 20-22 below for other key writings from which
this treatment of Weber is drawn.

16. Troeltsch, *The Social Teaching of the Christian Churches* (New York:
Harper, 1931).

17. Tawney, *Religion and the Rise of Capitalism* (New York: Harcourt,
Brace, 1926).

18. See, for example, Jürgen Moltmann, *The Experimental Hope* (Philadelphia: Fortress Press, 1975), especially chap. 9; and Juan Luis Segundo, *The
Liberation of Theology,* trans. John Drury (Maryknoll, N.Y.: Orbis Books, 1976),
especially pp. 19ff.

had criticized them on just that point. Few alternative "scientific" views, however, were at hand to deal with the relationship of religion to political power and economic change. To be sure, both Smith and Marx believed in a kind of "providence," evident in the "laws" of economic development that, if properly followed, would inexorably lead society to a noble, harmonious, benevolent, efficient, and humane future. They thought they had discovered these laws by asking similar questions. Smith was curious why some nations were wealthier than others, and wanted to know what produced wealth. Marx wanted to know why some classes of people were poor, and how the laws of economic history might remedy this condition. Smith believed that the answers could be found in the "invisible hand" of the market, and Marx thought that they could be seen in the "dialectics" of the class struggle.

Weber and his followers, however, doubted whether it is possible to read any pattern of moral improvement directly from the laws by which political economies have developed. Weber saw the relationship of "is" and "ought" as much more complex than Smith and Marx thought it to be. God is not the world, Providence is not necessarily what happens in social history by the "natural laws" of either evolution or revolution, and moral principles are distinct from the findings of the empirical sciences about how things work. Indeed, if we join them too quickly, each may distort an accurate understanding of the other. The "facts" of a social phenomenon do not prove its ethical or spiritual validity, and the most profound moral commitment cannot guarantee an accurate reading of the way things are in the world. There may well be "natural laws" that govern the way material reality works. But even if we knew them fully, there is still an "other" level of meaning and value that cannot be explained by them.

This distinction between "fact and value" is one of the things that has made Weber subject to the sharpest criticisms from the right and left wings of social thought, both of which want to read values from facts and facts from values in a closed hermeneutical circle. Weberians think that the circle is always open, and that therefore theology and the social sciences cannot be collapsed into one another, nor can one displace the need for the other. "Christian sociology" and "social ethics," insofar as they have any validity in guiding public decision-making, are always "synthetic" and are to be heeded only insofar as they meet the *double* test of accurate interpretation of the dynamics and structures of society, and reliable knowledge of the source and norm of ethical first principles.

The theologian as theologian has no special competence in the former, and the social theorist as social theorist has none in the latter.
Neither a normative nor a descriptive account of political economic
change is sufficient by itself.

But this does not mean that fact and value have nothing to
do with one another in social history. Indeed, one of the chief contributions of Weber and others who work in a comparable way is
that they have demonstrated by historical and comparative analysis
that each level impacts on the other in forming specific constella-
tions of political and economic life. The theological level, when
believed by the people and routinized into the fabric of society,
shapes the motivations of individuals and masses. The religious,
moral, and spiritual commitments that people have are themselves
"cultural" facts of social importance that introduce new and unpredictable patterns of living into political and economic existence.
The economic or political sciences can trace, by typological comparison and contrast, the characteristic ways in which this "other"
level interacts with the more or less predictable patterns of economic and political development and alters them by changing social
patterns of human actions, human relationships, and the relationships of human groups to material and political forces. At the same
time, the groups who are attracted to a specific spiritual or moral
perspective and who adopt and adapt it to their material needs also
influence the specific shape of a religious tradition. People are always driven by both "ideal interests" and "material interests." And
it is possible to investigate the mutual interaction of such influences, although such an investigation plunges us into the enormous
complexity of social and cultural history, where all neat schemes
of political and economic change according to clearly predictable,
empirically derived laws break down.

It is true, of course, that business managers and political
commissars (as well as numerous economists) have followed Smith
or Marx or their heirs, and that public political-economic debates
continue to be conducted very much in these terms. It is also the
case that a number of modern theologians who have newly discovered the "social question" are immediately more attracted to the
heirs of Smith or Marx than to the heirs of Weber. It wonderfully
simplifies life if we think that understanding the situation tells us
also what we ought to do, so that we do not have to worry about
theological or ethical questions; or if we think that knowing what
ought to be done theologically gives us privileged insight into the
situation without our having to do any research.

However, a minority tradition attempting to reconstruct "Christian sociology" has moved in other directions. Leading social theorists of the post-World War II period such as Robert MacIver, Talcott Parsons, Robert Merton, Reinhart Bendix, S. N. Eisenstadt, Robert Bellah, and Clifford Geertz have all tended to move away from either Smith or Marx and toward a "Weberian" position. They recognize that theological convictions have a social reality and importance not reducable to material factors, although they have material effects. Leading Christian social ethicists have also worked in this general direction. The post-World War II generation of clergy-ethicists—led by Richard and Reinhold Niebuhr, John Bennett, James Luther Adams, Liston Pope, and Walter Muelder—have all taken major themes from the new methods of "historical, comparative sociology." Social and material factors of life have a dynamic of their own and cannot be grasped simply by theological insight, although they influence religion in every age.

The main point of this "school" of work is that modern economic developments cannot be understood simply on the basis of an analysis of material forces alone. Inevitably, "ideal" forces, when "routinized" and institutionalized in an ethos by interaction with material forces, produce major shifts in societies and history. Material forces alone seldom if ever bring about any enduring change to political economy. And if that is the case, attentiveness to the kind and quality of cultural, religious, and ethical values that come to pervade a social ethos is both analytically and normatively demanded.

Let us take, for example, the material impulse to acquire and dominate, which has existed in every epoch of history and in every culture known to humankind. It has no special relation to modern industrial societies. Indeed, cultures other than Western cultures have frequently experienced this impulse. They also have or have had many of the political and technological preconditions for the development of modern economic systems. Yet they have not so developed, as Smith and Marx and their disciples who held to a model of *homo economicus* would have expected. They have not done so because modern economic systems have behind them a particular, methodical attitude toward the world. That attitude involves specific forms of discipline, restraint, and planning, and the intentional organization of means and ends. In short, modern economic systems have the material interests and the social preconditions *and* a specific "ascetic" attitude toward the world that "greed" cannot explain. This "rationalizing" attitude, the basis of all "modernization," Weber calls the "spirit" of modern political economies; we commonly call it "capitalism."

Before we proceed, a word needs to be said about the meaning of the word "capitalism," even though our focus will be on what is meant by its "spirit." Because of the long debates about the relative merits of capitalism and socialism, it is commonly believed that Weber is here referring to laissez-faire economic patterns of life. In addition, because of the legacy in theological circles of the Social Gospel in America and of religious socialism in Europe, and because of the impact of Marx on liberation theology in contemporary postcolonial nations, the common assumption is that Weber is contrasting capitalism and socialism. There is some modest merit for this view, insofar as Weber clearly refers to entrepreneurial activity in the eighteenth and nineteenth centuries, but that is obviously not his main point. His major purpose is not to contrast capitalism and socialism in these senses. It is to distinguish between, on the one hand, modern, rationalized modes of production and distribution that use technological means and are centered in bureaucratized institutions and governed by "rational-legal" forms of authority, and, on the other hand, traditional economies that are centered in familial institutions of clan, tribe, or caste, and based on methods of agriculture, craft, or manorial expropriation handed down from parents to children and governed by patriarchal authority. In short, his purpose is to contrast "modern" and "traditional" patterns of society. In view of *this* primary distinction, it is clear that the "capitalism" to which he is referring is any methodical, disciplined, social organization of human and material means of production geared to the accumulation of increased capital which is then rationally deployed to further enhance efficient production. Of course, this entails both constant social change and a willingness to transform traditional "communal" loyalties into new patterns of cooperative societal organization. This is the sort of social activity that is equally at home in corporate-capitalist and state-capitalist environments, the environments we usually have in mind when we refer to tensions between "capitalism" and "socialism." But this is not what Weber means.[19]

19. For examples of non-Western theologians who do engage in comparative and historical analysis and draw distinctions between theological and sociological patterns while relating them, see Choan-Seng Song, *Third-Eye Theology: Theology in Formation in Asian Settings* (Maryknoll, N.Y.: Orbis Books, 1979); Lamin Sanneh, *West African Christianity: The Religious Impact* (Maryknoll, N.Y.: Orbis Books, 1983); Kosuke Koyama, *Mount Fuji and Mount Sinai: A Critique*

Our central concern with Weber, however, has to do with the term "spirit" as it bears on modern political economies. In his view, modern socialist and capitalist political economies are both rooted in a worldview that is religious in origin and character. It is one of the primary examples of how a particular metaphysical-moral vision of the "other level" shaped persons and an entire ethos to alter the natural logic of political economy. In his study of ancient Judaism and early Christianity, Weber shows anticipations of this modern development in the "charisma" of the prophets, although traditionalist elements were still too pervasive.[20] The material foundations for modernization were often better developed in Hindu, Buddhist, Confucian, and Islamic cultures than in the West; but traditional religious and cultural values in these non-Western cultures, especially rigorous loyalties to familial and national "communities," prevented transformations to modern political economy — although aspects of Confucian thought had an ascetic work ethic and a high appreciation of business acumen.[21]

The transformation to modern political economies became a real possibility when specific branches of Protestantism saw work and the rational ordering of means and ends in production, distribution, finance, and technology as "meaningful" in an ultimate sense. "Natural" and "traditional" patterns of social life — economy, politics, family life, and patriarchal authority — could be transformed toward "modern" societal arrangements because humans have a vocation to do God's will in the world, a divinely given vocation to bring justice and righteousness and order to a fallen world where traditional patterns of moral convention (which seem to be natural laws) are in fact the sinful artifacts of human contrivance. Humankind is aided in this vocation by the careful, rational study of God's will, which is not opposed to the deeper forms of reason, and by the scientific study of the "laws of nature" that God wrote into the world in creation. On these bases, the social worlds of traditional communities, like the magical views of nature held by animists everywhere, are "de-mystified," and the transition to modernizing societies becomes possible.

---

of Idols (Maryknoll, N.Y.: Orbis Books, 1984); and, with more direct reference to Weber, Rubem Alves, *Protestantism and Repression* (Philadelphia: Westminster Press, 1985).

20. See Weber, *Ancient Judaism* (New York: The Free Press, 1952).

21. See Weber, *The Religion of China: Confucianism and Taoism*, trans. and ed. Hans Gerth (New York: The Free Press, 1951); and *The Religion of India*, trans. and ed. Hans Gerth (New York: The Free Press, 1958).

Weber, Troeltsch, and Tawney were quite alert to the fact that not all became deeply religious and then, on the basis of their convictions, consciously sought to change the world. On the contrary, many found that the changes taking place were quite beneficial in directly material ways. And many "became religious" in order to satisfy their material interests, while others found it necessary only to exercise their interests in a purely utilitarian fashion within the social, economic, and political systems this transformation brought about.[22] Very few worried much at all about any "other" level in any critical way, although all humans have to believe that their actions are "meaningful." Modern industrial societies — once the change had brought them about — could become purely "secular" in regard to these actions, as Benjamin Franklin's prudent advice in *Poor Richard's Almanac* already established for the rising middle classes in the West. For the workers and peasants of the vast underclasses of traditional communities, however, only the twentieth-century revolutions allowed the choice for "meaningful" modernization. Once such decisions are made, of course, they have to be implemented in systematic ways to become effective — in processes of "routinization," "institutionalization," and, with special reference to large-scale political and economic systems, "bureaucratization." Such processes have their own necessities.

Nevertheless, it is not possible to understand modern industrial societies, in contrast to all the "traditional" cultures of the world, without recognizing the hidden power of essentially religious orientations. Just as the economies of ancient China, India, Egypt, Israel, and the medieval West cannot be understood without reference to their religiously shaped worldviews, so the "rationalization" of modern economic life must be understood, at least in part, by reference to its religious rootage. The social ethos produced by the "elective affinity" of ideal and material factors has become a powerful and pervasive force in most of the "First" and "Second" Worlds. The historic conjoining of multiple religious and material forces has given rise to social forms of life that no "laws of the market" and no "dialectic of history" could grasp. It has produced an economic condition that today determines "the lives of all the

---

22. See Weber's shorter essay "The Protestant Sects and the Spirit of Capitalism," in *From Max Weber,* ed. Gerth and Mills (Oxford: Oxford University Press, 1947). See also R. H. Tawney, *The Acquisitive Society* (New York: Fontana Library, 1921); and Ernst Troeltsch, *Protestantism and Progress* (Boston: Beacon Press, 1958).

individuals who are born into ... [these] mechanism[s] ... ,"
whether or not they are consciously "religious" in any overt way.[23]

At present, the systems have lost their consciousness of a
theological dependency; they run by a utilitarian, secular calculus
that takes place within a seldom-examined set of presuppositions.
The absence of a metaphysical-moral grounding means that such
systems will either petrify, be met by "entirely new prophets," or
be transformed by a "great rebirth of old ideas and ideals." In short,
religion has been and may again be historically decisive for political
economies. Indeed, without an inner spiritual and ethical foundation, a political economy simply becomes an "iron cage."[24]

Those concerned with our political economy can see several
important clues to a viable stewardship in this analysis. It may
well be a basically accurate portrait of how things have come to be
as they are. As Weber made clear, we can no longer doubt the
relevance of theology to public matters, at least in having produced
our present state of affairs. Further, we can see in Weber's work
a way to avoid the traps of Smith and Marx. Both of these thinkers
removed religion from the realm of primary social causation. They
claimed that economic rationality was autonomous from religion,
an autonomy that Weber did not think could exist for long, even in
secularized societies. And finally, Weber's work shows us both the
relative epistemological independence and the inevitable social interdependence of religious ethics and political economy in human
history. It is for this reason that he can be called the Einstein of
modern social theory. Whatever criticisms might be properly lev-
eled at Weber, Troeltsch, Tawney, and their heirs, it remains the
case that theologians, social analysts, religious ethicists, and
"Christian sociologists" who debate economic issues with primary
reference to Adam Smith or Karl Marx (and their heirs) appear to
be hopelessly trapped in outdated ideological cages where things
as they are and things as they ought to be get terribly confused.

THE NECESSARY ETHICAL TRANSFORMATION OF
WEBERIAN THEORY

Of course, a great gulf remains between the Christian authors and
the Weberian school of thought. Weber (and, to a large degree,
Troeltsch and Tawney) offered *descriptive* analyses of socioeco-

---

23. Weber, *The Protestant Ethic and the Spirit of Capitalism*, p. 181.
24. Weber, *The Protestant Ethic and the Spirit of Capitalism*, p. 181.

nomic matters and of the roles that religious and ethical values play in comparative and historical cultures. But all who are interested in a public theology are primarily interested also in *normative* questions. The specific responsibility of religious leadership and institutions is to offer reliable, warranted guidance about how we *ought* to believe as we face social realities. On this point Weber cannot help us. He is not a theologian or an ethicist. He has demonstrated that modern social realities simply cannot be understood without detailed knowledge of the metaphysical-moral visions that, along with other factors, brought into existence the modern ethos, on which our political and economic systems depend. But he cannot tell us whether that metaphysical-moral system is true or just.

Increasingly it can be recognized that precisely the ethos that Weber identified has catalyzed an almost overwhelming internationalization of modernization of the world, to the great distress of the elders in every traditional culture and of the romantics in our own. Not only has this ethos transformed major features of Europe and North America; it has penetrated Asia, Africa, and South America, even if the official versions of the origins and value foundations of modernization were and are oblivious to or hostile to the religious and ethical constraints that engendered and guide them.

Great questions confront us as we face the present and the future. The structures of modern political economy have become ignorant of the inner logic that drives them. And if we cannot recover, refine, and recast the "spiritual" foundations, the rudderless mechanisms of modernity will increasingly become meaningless, purposeless, and unprincipled.

Today a number of ecumenical voices are again attempting to articulate the foundations of a public theology for modern political economies. The recent "pastoral letters" of the United States and Canadian Catholic bishops represent efforts to identify public theological principles by which modern corporate and state capitalisms can be addressed. Similarly, the United Presbyterian Church of the United States and the United Church of Christ have prepared new statements on theology and economic responsibility. These suggestive new efforts are worthy of extensive study. But it is not yet clear whether a serious metaphysical-moral vision can be developed that accords with both the deepest and broadest ecumenical theological tradition and a viable social analysis of political economy. The remainder of this book will be devoted to suggesting some possible next steps.

Study Questions

This chapter notes the developments the churches have been challenged to address since the articulation of a "Christian sociology" — the "rationalization" of political and economic life around the world, terrors such as Stalinism and Fascism, and the new voices from the "Third World."

1. What problems result from the "rationalization" of society if it is not based on a theological foundation? What benefits of "rationalization" do we want to honor?

2. Given the presence of sin in the world, will there ever be a government that ultimately will not be self-destructive? Should religious people therefore avoid all political entanglements?

3. God's Kingdom is not a democracy. How is it, then, that democracy is thought to more closely reflect God's purposes on earth than other social systems?

4. Over the centuries, Christians have been torn between pacifism and participation in militant action. How does a public theology affect the Christian's involvement in war?

5. What is the relationship, if any, between material (financial) development and spiritual and moral development?

6. Has your faith been influenced by your "material interests"? How does this differ from idolatry?

7. Do you think such ecumenical organizations as the World Council of Churches have aided in the understanding of our stewardship of modern political and economic institutions?

8. Do you think that modern corporations are too much or too little controlled by political authority? Do you think modern politics is too much or too little controlled by the interests of the corporations?

9. Do you agree that the economic theories of Adam Smith and Karl Marx are too trapped in the particular circumstances of earlier times to be of any use today? Can we learn anything useful and compatible with Christianity from either of them? If so, what?

10. Do you agree that it is better to have "a social theory of politics and economics" than "an economic theory of politics and society"? Why?

11. Max Weber and others believed that modern economic systems have an identifiable "spirit" that distinguishes them from "traditional" economies. Do you agree? Is that "spirit" compatible with Christianity?

12. Does "modernization" bring with it new perils and new promises to humanity and society? What are they? What place should be given to "traditional" economic attitudes and systems in the midst of a rapidly modernizing global economy made up of increasingly interdependent economic systems?

13. How do you think a Christian public theology ought to view various "scientific" debates about modern economics and politics? How does the description of "the way things are" influence your view of "how things ought to be"?

CHAPTER SIX

Piety
and
Power

So far we have pursued two lines of inquiry into resources for
public theology and its possible relationships to political economy — one systematic and the other historical. In the first, we identified the primary area of stewardly responsibility as the stewardship
of the Word, the *message,* which is at once faithful, coherent, and
capable of guiding thought and life in the face of modern existence.
I attempted to show that we must clarify the Word by use of the
interactive resources of Scripture, Tradition, Reason, and Experience. These are the touchstones of authority for all we have to say
and to do. When we take these points of reference as normative
and attempt to use them to identify the ways in which our understanding of the Word is to be enfleshed in the common life, we find
it both necessary and possible to develop a "public theology." Such
a theology addresses public issues; it makes sense in public discourse beyond the privileged insights of our confessional commu-
nions; and it offers answers of compelling substance to those
perennial and universal questions that must be addressed in every
age by every religion, philosophy, or metaphysical-moral worldview. The basic themes of Christianity — Creation, Liberation, Vocation, Covenant, Moral Law, Sin, Freedom, Church, Trinity, and
Christology — constitute the core concepts of a viable "science of
the divine" as it bears on public life. These themes carry rich resources for guiding society, and the stewardship of these themes is
the primary public responsibility of the church. These themes also
drive us to ethical engagement.

Through the historical focus of the preceding chapters, we have traced the ways in which Christians in the past century have applied these themes to a modern system of political economics as it emerged in the West and expanded around the globe. Their efforts evoked a "Christian sociology" that linked theological themes to modern institutions and gained ecumenical endorsement. However, contemporary structures of political economies — although they increasingly dominate the world — seem to have lost their inner metaphysical-moral foundations; the predominant models drawn from Adam Smith and Karl Marx and their heirs are incapable of providing the descriptive or normative grasp of these structures that is needed; and much of contemporary theology has become so confessional or contextual that it is incapable of giving warranted guidance to modernity. The theological right still depends on Smith, and the theological left turns increasingly to Marx; both become trapped in outmoded models that distort the analysis of society and of theology itself. Many of us in the churches today have become unsure about how to address the systems we face. Clearly, the concerns that drove the founders of "Christian sociology" have to be taken up again and linked to the basic motifs of a public theology under changed conditions.

With these foundations in mind, we turn to certain highly disputed questions in the area of political economy. Let us note at the outset, however, that there is always *both* much mutual influence *and* a notable difference between "politics" and "economics." The two are not the same, and there is always tension between them. To be sure, one is severely damaged when the other fails, and the health of one bodes well for the well-being of the other. Even more, the interests of one inevitably shape the actions of the other. But the little gap between the two terms in the phrase "political economy" symbolizes the fact that the two are not the same and that one of the greatest questions of modernity is how large that gap should be.

Further, neither "politics" nor "economy" is itself a single concept. In the context of modern life, for example, to speak of "the economy" means to refer not only to the processes of production and distribution, the laws of supply and demand, and the functions of the market, but also to a whole series of social institutions that cut the channels in which the economy runs. Indispensable to modern economies are complex legal systems, corporations, sophisticated technologies of management and communication, and the development of a new pluralism of professions. In the following chapters we will treat each of these in some detail. For now, let us simply note that where these are not well-developed, the only means at hand for controlling an economic structure are thought to be political, as the revolutionary governments of the left and the military governments of the right know. Yet complex legal systems, corporate institutional life, modern technologies, and professionalism seem to develop rapidly and creatively only in those kinds of social environments where political institutions do not control everything.

It is possible that our ordinary ways of understanding public life are deficient, that they are lacking precisely insofar as we understand public life essentially in political and economic terms. And it is possible that a social and theological interpretation can offer a more adequate reading of our modern situation *and* give us moral guidance as to how we ought to deal with it. At stake is not only the relation of politics to economy, but the basic values of modern civilization.

THE MULTIPLE FACETS OF POLITICAL POWER

Let us begin our analysis by trying to understand something of the nature of politics. Politics, at its core, is about power. It is about the accumulation, consolidation, and exercise of the capacity to give commands and to have those commands obeyed. The commands may take the form of laws, edicts, or policies; they may be formulated by kings, military elites, charismatic theocrats, revolutionary parties, or representative parliaments; and they may be more or less benevolent, humane, reasonable, and just, or precisely the opposite. But whatever forms are followed, whoever issues them, and however ethical their content, dynastic successions, elections, conquests, caucuses, alliances, *coups d'état,* and political parties are all efforts to get, to consolidate, and to exercise the power of command in a territory. When power is gained, organized forms of enforcement, agencies, police forces, and bureaucracies are either taken over or constructed to implement and enforce the commands. Insofar as power moves closer to implementation and enforcement, it always has behind it elements of coercion and force, even if these were not present (as they often are) in the gaining of power. If the law or the order is not followed, the courts, the agents of the state, or even the army will pursue the violator(s) with the threat of violence.

Because modern Western countries have experienced relatively peaceful transitions of power from leader to leader and party to party — a luxury in the history of politics and in most of the world today — those who live in constitutional democracies have tended to become blind to the hard fact that politics always has its forceful, coercive, and even lethal side. Around the world and in most of history, power passes hands only when blood is shed. To think about politics without paying attention to its coercive side is utterly naive.

I stress this point at this juncture for the simple reason that politics inevitably involves actions that every profound religion considers sinful. Politics uses violence, but does so to establish an order whereby violence is constrained. Believers thus always feel ambivalent about politics. At best, it can preserve us from worse violence and chaos and provide a relatively peaceful environment where other human activities can be given a chance to occur without violent disruption.

Religion is not, in the first instance, about politics. The Power that concerns religion is not the power of coercion. Nor is profound religion territorial, as politics inevitably is. Even if some religions seem at times to focus on some specific national territory — Zionist Judaism on Israel, Shiite Islam on Iran, Shintoism on Japan — there is something in the impulse of profound religion that knows that what is truly divine cannot be limited to, exhausted by, or fully enforced within any specific geographical limits or by methods of coercion. The attempts to do so, in fact, lead to imperialistic attempts to expand the boundaries of religion by expanding the regime. But that does not convict the heart.

The core of religion is piety, in the classical meaning of that term, and power and piety are simply not the same thing. Therefore, they are properly organized into two distinct communities in which people may participate. In modern (Western) vocabularies, we call one "state" and we call the other "church." It is important to note that these designations are *organizational* and *institutional* in character. However closely the Brahmanic priests and Kshatriya rulers cooperate in Hinduism, however much the Buddhist monks are supported by Buddhist kings, however intimate the imams of Islam are to caliphs, and whatever the linkages are between the sacerdotal offices of Christian clergy and the temporal rulers, a distinction is always drawn. Concretely, this means that membership and participation in the community of piety are not, cannot be, and ought not be determined by our membership and participation in the political order, or the other way around.

In the history of Christianity, this has been a major theme at least since the Wise Men came to worship a King that the king knew not of and since Christ instructed us to "Render unto Caesar the things that are Caesar's, and unto God the things that are God's." To be sure, this theme has been obscured in parts of the Christian tradition where the church became established as a territorial church. Yet it has been preserved wherever the church has reached across national lines to establish communities on other grounds, and has attempted to establish principles of justice that are used to evaluate every political system and ideology. The direct political results of this are many and complex. They cannot be fully traced here. But in a long and multifaceted history, the implications are clear: Our religious membership ought not to depend on whether we belong to the "correct" political organization or are citizens of the "right" political order as decided by some sectarian authority.[1]

Efforts to weave piety and power into a single fabric never work for long. In both the political and religious traditions that have shaped the West, both of which have grown out of a very profound public theology, we have decided that it is wrong to try to effect this synthesis. The separation of church and state is one of our most precious legacies from the past. It is the well-warranted conviction — rooted also in Scripture, Reason, and Experience — that both politics and religion suffer if either church or state commits its destiny into the hands of the other by making one into the other or by making one a tool to get a purchase on the other. Since World War II, more and more of the world's nations have come to share this conviction, although it is not an integral part of their religious histories. It is a point enshrined in the United Nations Declaration of Human Rights, and it is now stated in principle in most of the constitutions of the affiliated nations, although it is in practice frequently violated.

But the separation of church and state is not the whole story. Institutional arrangements, however important, do not exhaust the meanings of religion and politics or of piety and power. Power and piety are not simple realities but complex ones, and we have not

---

1. I have discussed these matters at some length in my book *Creeds, Society, and Human Rights: A Study in Three Cultures* (Grand Rapids: Eerdmans, 1984), especially in chaps. 1-6. This view contrasts with some currently influential "radical" views that are quite sectarian. See, for example, Beverly Harrison, *Making the Connections: Essays in Feminist Social Ethics*, ed. Carol Robb (Boston: Beacon Press, 1985).

yet touched on some of the complexities. We need to take our reflections further and draw deeper conclusions.

As we have already noted, power has one side that always
includes an element of coercion and violence. But that is not all
that it has. Money is also power — although in a different sense.
Wealth is a high-potency *influence* that can distort both piety and
political life. It always plays a role in politics. People of wealth are
disproportionately influential in every power constellation, even if
many civilized states try to keep that influence under control. The
means of doing this are many and varied. In democratic lands, for
example, it is morally and legally wrong to buy and sell votes.
Wherever votes are purchased, a practice that is not unusual among
populations not yet democratized, the distinction between political
and economic systems is not yet secure. Even where the distinction
is accepted, however, influence peddling is widely practiced. And
political regimes around the world attempt to insure their duration
by fostering those conditions that allow the citizenry — or at least
some segments of it — to improve their material condition. In Western democracies there are also restrictions on lobbyists and the
amounts that any individual can give to a particular campaign,
although there are intense debates as to how effective these controls
are and whether or not they are strict enough. Clearly, elected officials who take bribes, sell appointments to offices, or auction
votes on key legislative issues are thieves, subject to exposure and
prosecution.

These simple observations point to a larger problem that will
crop up in the remaining chapters as well. Although there exist
some very important moral, legal, and institutional distinctions between politics and economics, we must recognize the inevitable
relationship between political power and economic influence. The
naive notion that there should be an *absolute* distinction between
politics and economy, as held by the theorists of laissez-faire economics, can simply not be sustained. For one thing, governments
print or coin the money upon which the whole of modern economic
activity depends. For another, the laws protecting private economic
activity and property are laws passed and enforced by political
authority. And, for still another, governments do not generate their
own financial resources. They must rely on taxes, collected under
threat of coercive action, if they are to provide the roads, the bridges,
and the waterways on which commerce, trade, and industry depend. Even more, economic activity presumes a degree of relative
peace. Economies collapse in the midst of war. Investment flees

conflict. Business, which lives by calculations geared to a reliable future, cannot plan when political order breaks down. To be sure, there are always those munitions manufacturers, army suppliers, and military contractors who reap great fortunes in times of unrest, but they make up a relatively small part of any viable economy.

Perhaps we can see some implications of these social facts even at this point. While the laissez-faire ideology brooks no connection between political and economic sectors of society and thus falsifies the actual and necessary fact of relationship between politics and economics, there is also the opposite danger — that of fully integrating political and economic institutions. That, as Reinhold Niebuhr pointed out years ago, is one of the greatest perils of a Marxist economy.[2] In Marxist-Leninist societies, efforts to overcome the disproportionate influence of the wealthy few on political life lead to an attempt to control economic activities politically. However, since economies do not operate entirely by political logics but by the interaction of political, technological, social, cultural, and religious factors, political power must move to control the total social system to control the economy. This not only establishes vast bureaucracies of control but also creates a new elite class instead of promoting the classless political economy desired. Our present focus does not allow further analysis of this reality. What we can note at this point, however, is that Marxist-influenced liberationist movements that pursue this direction today have been no more successful than laissez-faire ideologies at identifying the simultaneous independence and interdependence of political and economic life.

Power has other dimensions as well. Style is one of them. Attractive style consolidates power, although what counts as "attractive" includes cultural and subcultural aesthetics. Hannah Tillich reported that it was style that attracted the German masses to Hitler, and that the first signs of opposition to Hitler came not on the basis of assessments of his policies but on the basis of contempt among "cultured" people for his style.[3] And in the modern context of elaborate mass media, style seems to increase in importance. In the American context, style includes "ethnic elements." The patterns of speech, rhetoric, gesture, and symbol give a wide range of signals about whether or not a candidate, a leader, or a party is

---

2. See Niebuhr, "The Christian Faith and the Economic Life . . . ," in *Goals of Economic Life,* ed. A. D. Ward (New York: Harper, 1953).

3. Tillich, *From Time to Time* (New York: Stein & Day, 1974).

empathetic to Yankees, Blacks, Jews, Italians, Irishmen, Asians, or Hispanics. The questions of male and female balances in style and visible leadership will increasingly influence political power as well. But behind these questions of style are often assessments of piety, the question of whether or not this candidate or party or movement is deeply and genuinely committed to those metaphysical-moral visions that are most deeply held by those who must assess the potential holders of political power.

In addition, brains count in power — both in terms of the intelligence of leaders and in terms of their capacities to attract good minds into their camps. Nobody admires stupid leadership. All political aspirants attempt to convince the public, especially the opinion makers, that they understand the issues, that they have the knowledge, the "smarts," to handle complex issues, and that they can attract the best minds to their cause — unlike the opposition, which is portrayed as ignorant or foolish. And again piety enters the picture, for people put their confidence only in leaders who show evidence of a deeper kind of intelligence — a certain sagacity that is more than mastery of data, command over information, or approval by honored experts. People will support those aspirants to political power who show a capacity for "spiritual wisdom."

But power is more complex still. Political power not only involves force, the influence of wealth, the attraction of style, and the facility of brains; political power also wants and needs the belief among the governed that it has the right to command these things. It needs agreement that it *ought* to rule, that controlling these things is *legitimate.* Style and wisdom contribute to this, but so does law. People will resist political power if it violates established legality in getting or using power, or if it uses style and smarts to deviate from the law. In every contest over power, there are charges and countercharges that properly promulgated laws have been violated. Here we must see that one of the basic themes of public theology comes into play. Power requires legitimacy, and the first mark of such legitimacy is its obedience to law. But just at this point we must emphasize that it is not simply the law of the land that is at stake, for everyone knows that unjust laws can be passed and enforced coercively for at least a while. It is a matter of "moral law," a vision of basic principles of right and wrong that are behind or embodied in those laws, which are to be obeyed even by those who pass laws, issue edicts, and give commands. And if those who have political power do not follow *these* laws, rising tides of conspirators will attempt to disobey the law, to evade its enforcement, to resist those who enforce it, and to challenge and eventually overthrow the political powers who make the law.

What is at stake here is the question of "authority." If some political group, party, or leader is going to be accorded political power in the long run, the authority of moral and spiritual factors beyond the letter of the law is inevitably involved. At this point, piety at its deepest and broadest levels shapes political possibility. This is the least tangible aspect of power, but it is perhaps the most potent.

The failure to recognize this fact is one of the great failures of much contemporary theology that tries to be politically relevant — and perhaps of many modern political theories generally. Many have thought that in dealing with power, they are only being realistic if they become more Machiavellian. But this concentration on "realistic" analysis, on the hard calculations of who holds sway over the guns, dollars, brains, and law, has contributed to the creation of a vacuum at the moral and spiritual level on this question of legal authority.[4] Into that vacuum are flooding the new fanaticisms of the right and the left, often under the labels of fundamentalism and liberationism. They are struggling for control over the piety of the people. Both fundamentalists and liberationists know, better than most ecumenically oriented believers, that this is a decisive arena for the shape of power. We are here at the doorstep of moral and spiritual authority, and the shape of the dominant piety will shape the future of power as much as any other single factor. This is precisely the point at which the relationship of Scripture, Tradition, Reason, and Experience also appears (see Chapter One).

In sum, power in its deeper and more complex dimensions requires religious authority. Although it is necessary to separate church and state at one level because piety and power are not about the same thing, at this level religion and politics inevitably overlap. Indeed, politics requires religion. The critical question politically is what kind and quality of religion will come to dominate. And that critical question also demands posing the question of what kind and quality of religion ought to dominate. That question requires

---

4. See L. Menaud, "Critical Legal Studies: Radicalism for Yuppies," *New Republic,* 17 March 1986, pp. 20ff. A deeper, broader study that treats the historic relationship between normative theological and ethical concerns and the formation of constitutional rules of law is H. J. Berman, *Law and Revolution: The Formation of the Western Legal Tradition* (Cambridge: Harvard University Press, 1983).

a theological answer, one for which public warrants can be given. A public theology is required, and all who wish to become stewards of modern political economies have to become theologians in this sense, whether they want to or not, because theology is the only science that critically evaluates divergent pieties and investigates whether or not any of them are based on the warranted knowledge of divine things, as they claim to be.

PIETY'S RELATIONSHIP TO POLITICS: SOME LIMITS

We can look at these same questions from the standpoint of piety as well as from the side of power. The core of profound religion is the relationship of the soul to God and to other souls in a community of faith. It is on this basis that we establish religious organizations. The decision to participate in worship, prayer, and mutual care is, in one very profound sense, intensely personal and not at all political. In some senses, however, it is not a private "decision" at all. We feel ourselves grasped by a power greater than we are—one that bonds us to people we would not otherwise find among our friends, people with whom we do not otherwise share interests. This power leaps over boundaries and barriers of force, wealth, style, brains, and territorial laws to direct us in pursuit of ends and to bring us under principles that we ourselves could not have constructed or chosen—principles of righteousness, purpose, and compassion that no human can control. To be sure, much of this is and remains private, and something of it is betrayed when it becomes politicized. Indeed, when religious groups become obsessed with questions of power—either internally, in "church fights," or externally, when only those who are of one or another political loyalty are considered brothers and sisters in faith—something irretrievable is lost in piety.

Still, that is not the whole story, because as soon as people take their piety seriously, as soon as it becomes the rock upon which they build the foundations of their lives, as soon as God is seen as the true and vital guide to the whole of existence, piety refuses to remain private only. It reaches out and transforms attitudes and behavior with regard to wealth, wisdom, and law. It also transforms our understanding of style and moves toward cosmopolitan perspectives in questions of nationality, ethnicity, class, and gender. No longer are force, wealth, style, brains, and civil law the marks of final meaning. Power based on these is deprived of ultimate significance, although these become arenas of stewardly responsibility in society under standards derived from a source that must be examined and understood in terms of the science appropriate to it — theology.

When these concerns become incarnated in life, they bring social change, and they transform the ethos on which political life depends. They reshape our sense of the good society, of a right polity, of national priorities, and of public policy. If a piety that can stand the test of theological scrutiny is taken seriously, it speaks to public as well as private questions, to political as well as personal issues, although its primary concern is never politics. It demands a righteousness and a justice, a peace and a compassion that influence politics through the consciences of believers and through careful ethical witness on the part of the community of faith for the sake of humanity. Thus every profound piety reaches beyond itself and demands responsible political engagement even though it knows that politics is not the core meaning of life, and that we are finally neither damned nor saved by political power. Earlier we saw that a deeper analysis of power reveals that politics requires religion, and here we see by a deeper analysis of piety that religion requires social engagement that will have political consequences.

It is impossible and nonsensical to think that, at this level — which is different from the institutional level of church and state — religion and politics will not be intertwined. If religion does not have implications at this level of social ethics, it is either a false or an immature religion. Indeed, one reason for the separation of church and state at the other level is that it allows religion to form its influence in the piety of the people free from state control. Another reason is that piety, through the conscience of the people and the free organization of religious groups, can serve as a check on governmental tyranny over those fundamentally religious, ethical, spiritual, and moral commitments, rooted in piety, where no politician, state, party, or government has special competence, right, or privilege.

Since it is the case that a deeper grasp of power and piety requires a separation of church and state at one level and an intimate relationship of religion and politics at another, we can now be more specific about a number of areas where the relationships and distinctions interface and threaten to undo one another. Let me review six of these areas that have great practical implications for the practice of stewardship in our modern political economy.

First, a very important distinction between sin and crime

must be maintained. Some things, such as murder, robbery, rebellion, and rape, are in fact both sinful and criminal. Those who are pious will avoid sin in these areas and will obey and cooperate with state authorities who must, at times, use coercion to control these crimes. But not all issues are so simple. Sometimes killing — for instance, a soldier's killing an enemy in a war — may not be criminal. Indeed, the state may require us to pay for, train for, or actually engage in killing as a civic duty. Ordinarily, if a war is unavoidable and justifiable in terms of the prevention of a more horrendous evil, responsible people may remain faithful believers and dutiful citizens and participate in the killing — even if they, as believers, know that the whole situation that made the war necessary is sinful and should have been avoided or rectified before it required such a grim remedy. Similarly, if political power — as a combination of force, wealth, style, and brains — passes laws that violate universal principles of justice such as human rights, oppresses profound piety, and destroys the institutional separation of church and state, believers may be morally and spiritually required to participate in revolution.

At other moments, when exploitative powers control political life or when weapons that threaten humanity, society, and creation are commanded, it may be sinful to take up arms even if the state requires it and punishes, as criminals, those who refuse to do so. In such situations, believers may be called upon to risk criminal prosecution for the sake of avoiding sin. Of course, such decisions always require concrete social analysis of the actual situation and attention to the first principles of a public theology. This is the basic logic behind the pastoral letter on nuclear war drawn up by the U.S. Roman Catholic bishops.[5] Whether one agrees with all its findings is less important than the fact that it presents a viable, warranted, public theological statement on these matters unmatched by any other church statement on this issue in the twentieth century.

Closely related to this first issue is the second one: the matter of *who* is to define what is sinful and *who* is to define what is criminal. Usually these distinctions are left to religious leadership and political leadership respectively. And this means that the proper relationship of religious leaders and political leaders is an indirect relationship, not a direct one. Of course, clergy must be free to

---

5. See *The Challenge of Peace: God's Promise and Our Response* (Ramsey, N.J.: Paulist Press, 1983).

speak out on public moral issues, and politicians may properly state which faith commitments are most important to them. But clergy ought not to become officers of state and take on the vestments of coercive authority in crime and punishment. Likewise, political officers ought not to become the definers of proper religious rite, ritual, sacrament, doctrine, attitude, or action.

We can express this indirect relationship another way. Clergy and politicians must work through the consciences of the people. Believer-citizens must decide, in dialogue and debate with others within and beyond the community of faith, which principles and perspectives taught by clergy are to be taken with utmost seriousness and which with a grain of salt, and which policies of politicians are worthy of support and which demand throwing the rascals out. We all make such assessments, and we need to acknowledge overtly how valid they are. It is believer-citizens who must decide how to be stewards of piety's principles and perspectives as they apply to actual material conditions — matters in which laity may be quite as knowledgeable as the clergy. This entails, of course, a very high sense of vocation for the laity and a specialized role for the clergy. The clergy have the responsibility, as teachers and preachers in the midst of the people, to offer a public theology that articulates the basic principles governing life, and to relate that theology to a "Christian sociology" that equips the people to interpret the moral and spiritual issues of the society. But laypersons are the ones who have to decide whether such preaching and teaching makes sense and how that should play out in concrete political decision-making. The teachings and preachings of clergy are to be followed only when they point to that which is genuinely authoritative, not when they claim special privilege.

The third area that stands at that delicate juncture of the two levels — that of the distinction between church and state and the relationship between religion and politics — is social service and social advocacy. When piety becomes articulate in a public theology, it will also become articulate in action and organization beyond the body of believers. It will develop voluntary associations that reach out and care for those neighbors by organizing support systems for them in a way that no individual can manage alone.[6] Further, it will attempt to alter those social institutions that stunt,

---

6. See J. L. Adams, *Voluntary Associations,* ed. J. R. Engel (Chicago: Exploration Press, 1986); and Robert Evans and H. C. Boyte, *Free Spaces: The Sources of Democratic Change* (San Francisco: Harper & Row, 1986).

oppress, or corrupt whole groups of people—especially by empowering those people to develop the means of overcoming their subjection.

To be sure, religious efforts along these lines have sometimes risen to such a level that an entire population has come to see that it has new responsibilities. Schools were once founded by the churches. So were hospitals, orphanages, and homes for the poor, the elderly, the incompetent, and the outcast. Many of these functions in modern political economies were subsequently taken over by government. It is not insignificant that all parties in modernized societies today presume that some forms of public education, welfare, social security, health and safety protection, and medical care will and must be services offered by the whole society through government—although there are all sorts of intense political debates about the degree of support these services should receive and whether or not some forms of the governmental programs do not cultivate a subculture of dependency. Today some argue that the major moral question before modern political economies is the question of degree. But it is more likely that the willingness of the churches to turn all such functions over to the government has meant that the moral and spiritual authority that called people to care for and support the disadvantaged has begun to decay. Consequently, government officials feel no great pressure from the population to be concerned about the disadvantaged. It may be that only renewed religious action in "charitable" fields will renew public commitment and again lay the groundwork for governmental assumption of responsibilities.

Religious organizations in the ecumenical traditions often also participate in the organized mobilization of the disadvantaged to see that common resources are made available to them in a maximal, generous way and not a minimal, grudging way. Whether or not this is the best strategy is not a matter of *basic* political principle but a matter of prudence in many situations. What is a matter of principle is that if people argue against government programs of this sort in favor of alternative, nongovernmental approaches to problems of systemic disadvantage *but* do not engage in the energetic voluntary pursuit of social service and social advocacy, they betray the marks of a genuine public theology that since biblical days has seen concern for the weak, the widows, and the oppressed as a mark of the pious life.

The fourth area of concern has to do with international affairs. Earlier we noted that all the great religions, and especially

Christianity, are not, in principle, territorial. A public theology refuses to take any nation-state with ultimate seriousness. Modern Christians have an obligation to vote, to participate in political parties, and to press for political systems where voting and political parties are allowed, although it becomes very perilous to both piety and politics if religious organizations become political parties or focus their energy on political participation alone. Furthermore, in many contexts, Christians may be justifiably patriotic, even if being so involves moral and spiritual danger. A public theology does not retreat to the monastery, withdraw into sectarian communes, think that confessional commentary against the wickedness of the world will suffice, or allow itself to become satisfied with familistic ministries in local communities. But it is idolatry to vote, participate in parties, and make all political judgments in terms of a primary loyalty to nation. Monastic, sectarian, confessional, and familistic theologies do recognize that such loyalties turn quickly into preoccupations with national security or class or racial interest, and that these are severe perils to piety and morality. But the solution they offer merely leaves the world to the vultures and fails to incarnate the Word in the messy, conflict-laden world of modern political economy. A singular preoccupation with "big" issues, they say, tends to restrict God to some small geographical domain. A public theology takes the opposite step: the "big" issues of national politics are not yet large enough for the only God worth worshiping.

A profound piety will be the spur to develop a public theology that reaches to the neighbor whom we do not know, in cultures we do not understand, in societies we do not approve, and under regimes we must oppose. It will also resist every attempt to make these global concerns only a part of the warp and woof of our own nationalistic interests. Such a theology takes humanity as its public, and it takes the enemy as a companion in dialogue and debate. The community of discourse becomes all those among humankind who are willing to discuss the most important things. To put the matter differently, such a piety is the mother of missions, outreach, education, medical care, disaster relief, and the bringing of hope to the hopeless. The theology of and for this public is universalistic in scope, and it will alter votes and the character of the parties in which Christians participate. It is concerned about universal human rights; it is active in the attempts to establish a universal just peace. It promotes by conversion and nurture the formation of churches and voluntary associations and base communities, the infrastructure for viable democratic participation of all peoples in the sharing of power and political responsibility in principled ways. And wherever nations, including our own, oppose or resist such developments, the vote and opposition parties will be mobilized to alter leadership and policies.

Such a view, of course, has implications for how believer-citizens assess the foreign policies of their home countries. They will not take the news releases of their political and military leaders as the gospel but will attend to what their missionaries and their partner churches around the world have to say about the real conditions among the people affected by their national policies. They will not doubt the basic responsibility of those in government and military service to prepare for the worst, but they will ever prod to open up possibilities of a more excellent way. And in every encounter with another culture or civilization, they will ask whether dimensions of that society are not also witnesses to the *logos* of God, bearing elements of value, insight, wisdom, and truth that are of potentially universal importance yet have been obscured or undiscovered by our own traditions. As soon as one takes these perspectives into account, political ideologies are altered. Force, wealth, brains, and civil law become less tools to possess and enhance "our" interests for national benefit than resources to be employed for a larger vision. The tremendous power of modern political economies is not an end coinciding with the national good, but a means to be employed in stewardly responsibility for the service and salvation of humankind. And rather than support those who serve "our" interests, believer-citizens will elect, support, and grant authority to those political leaders who are willing to deploy power to enhance these ends.

This brings us to the fifth area to note in that "buffer zone" between church and state at the institutional level and politics and religion at the higher level. In our exercise of political responsibility, we must be constantly attentive to both the inevitable interdependence and the necessary independence of political and economic life. A proper separation of political and economic institutions parallels the separation of church and state, although there is always interpenetration and mutual influence. Certain kinds of interpenetration and influence are theologically and ethically valid. Gross inequities of economic influence on political life will have to be politically and legally controlled; they are criminal as well as sinful. And the political mobilization of the economically dispossessed has to be undertaken so that governmental policies can redress just grievances. No laissez-faire economy can exist in pure form when such mobilization results in political democracy.

The other form of imbalance — political domination of economic life — leads to controls over all aspects of society. It destroys economic viability, forces the nationalization of economic institutions, puts the power of the gun and the influence of wealth in the same set of hands, makes all job-getting a matter of political correctness, and inevitably tends also to involve the control of all matters of intelligence, style, and piety within a geographical territory. The delicate balance required can be sustained only if discipline, restraint of greed, and a pervasive sense of stewardship for all people become a part of our political decision-making.

And finally, a public theology will press all who seek to work out its implications toward the formation of just constitutions. Issues of authority converge with issues of legitimacy. One of the closest conversation partners of public theology will be jurisprudence.[7] It will seek those "forms of grace" that give orderly legal fabric to political and economic activity. By the recent celebration of the bicentennial of the U.S. Constitution and the Canadian struggle with the transition from an unwritten to a written "constitution" through the "Charter of Rights," we in the West are reminded that it is necessary, in political affairs, to articulate and defend reliable structures of law to guide the exercise of power. We are also reminded that few contemporary theologies, focused as they are on confessional and contextual themes, are capable of doing this.

To put the matter quite concretely, what current theological orientations of substance can fail to rejoice when the vicious terror and torture of old tyrannies are overthrown in Iran, Nicaragua, and the Philippines, or challenged in South Africa? But what modern theology provides a vision of those "forms of grace" necessary to prevent a vicious new theocracy from coming to power in Iran, to resist the Sandinista's suspension of key civil rights and liberties in Nicaragua, to aid the new government in the Philippines in writing a new constitution, or to evoke a vision of possible reconstructive order among those who will be called upon to lead after the *kairos* comes to its full destiny in South Africa? A public theology, as it bears on political life, will become engaged in just such questions, and the debates about such matters will become an integral part of our stewardship of the Word in the world.

---

7. See the new periodical *The Journal of Law and Religion* for a creative new dialogue on this front.

In sum, as stewards of the Word that is to become enfleshed in life, we need first of all to cultivate an understanding of public theology. And when we bring that to bear on issues especially pertinent to stewardship, we find that we must address the critical issues of political economy. That, however, has many parts, as we can see when we distinguish some of the main levels of power in political life. Public theology implies both a separation of church and state and a simultaneous intimate link between religion and politics that are attentive to those patterns of authority that may be deemed "forms of grace." The boundaries between these levels are to be guarded by several areas of active engagement. To be sure, sorting out the key issues this way does not solve all questions of political economy, and we will address other matters shortly. But it does allow us to see that many of the discussions about religion and political life in the recent election are simpleminded and confused. This confusion, I fear, is likely to last a very long time in our common life, and clearing it up will require a long-term program of teaching, preaching, and example. But the future of democracy and human rights and the prospects for a just and lasting peace may depend much more on clarity about issues such as these than about many of the so-called "hot issues" that preoccupy our religious and political leadership. If issues such as these are not addressed, we may fumble our stewardship responsibilities, winning little policy battles here and there but failing to edify the church, our nations, the whole people of God, and humankind.

Study Questions

In this chapter and in those to come, we turn from a study of the systematic and historical foundations of a public theology as it has addressed issues of political economy in the past, to new proposals about the relationship of faith and politics.

1. Historically, from biblical times to the present, how large a gap has existed between piety and power?

2. How large a gap has existed between economics and politics? To what extent does the possession of wealth insure political power for an individual or a group? To what extent does politics influence economic activity and the accumulation and distribution of wealth? Do you think that anything has changed recently? Should it change?

3. What is the relationship between "freedom of religion" and the development of modern political economies?

4. Some Christians say, "God does not force us to do anything." If politics is about power, and power inevitably involves force or coercion, how should Christians view "power" in the light of Scripture? How do you understand John 1:12 (". . . to all who received him, . . . he gave power to become children of God")?

5. Society is replete with examples of both formal and informal structures of power. Give examples of power that is not directly related to government and wealth.

6. What leadership style a society finds attractive says something about its aesthetics. Does a society's favoring a certain leadership style also say something about that society's religious orientation?

7. How is the "separation of church and state" an application of the principle of "vocation"?

8. What happens if church, state, and corporation are too closely intertwined? What are some consequences evident in the world today?

9. Do you believe that people look for "spiritual wisdom" in their leaders? Is this the case in atheistic societies or in secular institutions where God is discounted as an influence on politics and economics?

10. What is the relationship of "spiritual wisdom" to the principles of "moral law"? To "legitimacy"?

11. Many clergy today, especially in minority communities, have dual vocations. Sometimes they serve in the political arena as well as in the church. Is this in conflict with the separation of church and state? Are the rules governing such service different for clergy and laity from the standpoint of the church? From the standpoint of the state?

12. Many public welfare institutions were initiated by the church and later taken over by the state. Because the state can spread the costs and benefits of such institutions over a larger number of people, it tends to provide more services more economically. However, the state agencies sometimes have the reputation of being cold, impersonal, uncaring, and unspiritual. What should the church do about this?

13. Piety based on nationalism can be destructive. So can politics based on the religious zeal of some faction. What are examples of these? Despite such pitfalls, Christians are called to be stewards of political life. What kinds of political participation and what kinds of patriotism are possible for those who believe in a Christian public theology?

CHAPTER SEVEN

Spirituality and the Corporation

As long as we can forecast the realistic probabilities of the future of modern societies, the economies connected to them will be mixed. Decision-making about, capitalization for, and management of production and distribution will be centered in the corporation, although governmental regulations, tax policies, expenditures, and contracting will shape and modulate corporate policies. It is not clear what precise mix of private and public control of the economy we will have, but "corporate capitalism" is likely to be the predominant social form of economic life in the foreseeable future. Both a fully planned economy managed by the state and an economy of individual entrepreneurs are highly unlikely. Indeed, where these exist around the world, economic stagnation tends to result. The modern corporation has out-employed, out-researched, out-produced, and out-distributed every other known social form of economic organization. It develops most extensively in pluralistic societies, and considerable evidence suggests that it is structurally necessary to a viable democracy.[1]

These facts are troubling to many theologically and ethically

---

1. *The Judeo-Christian Vision and the Modern Business Corporation,* ed. Oliver Williams and John Houck (Notre Dame: University of Notre Dame Press, 1982). See also *Corporations and the Common Good,* ed. Robert Dickie and Leroy Rouner (Notre Dame: University of Notre Dame Press, 1986); and *Christianity and Capitalism,* ed. Bruce Grelle and David Krueger (Chicago: CSSR Press, 1986).

concerned leaders. For many, the corporation is the embodiment of profit-oriented greed, a soul-less artifact that pollutes the environment, uproots people from their farms, closes plants, dislocates workers, promotes growing discrepancies between the rich and the poor, and, in its transnational form, invades other cultures and corrupts indigenous societies. It is, to some, the enemy of spiritual life and social responsibility.

Those who celebrate corporate capitalism for its rather marvelous material achievements and those who pillory it for its manifest horrors become the chief ideological advocates of capitalism or socialism. But the one frequently misunderstands the social fabric of modern economic reality by focusing too much on the individual, and the other by holding a political theory of all social life, a view that makes politics sovereign over all economic functions. Each may be correct in thinking that the other oversimplifies economic life. But it is not clear that either has accurately diagnosed the social character of this distinctive feature of modern political economies. A responsible stewardship of modern society demands that we wrestle anew with "the corporation."

POSSIBLE SOCIAL CENTERS OF ECONOMIC ORGANIZATION

Only seven possible social centers of economic organization exist. Economic life, like any other basic human activity, has to have some definable social location. The first possibility is that it could be, at least in theory, completely individualistic. But even Robinson Crusoe needed Friday, and complex economies require that many people work together in organized ways. While individuals always make economic decisions, and the cumulative effect of millions of individual decisions is of enormous importance in any economy, pure economic individualism remains an ideological fantasy in modern societies. The modern corporation, like the modern governmental bureaucracy, cannot abide radical individualism, nor individualists them.

Economic activity could be centered in families, which are often regarded as the "building blocks" of society. And it is true that familial patterns, especially in their extended forms of clan, tribe, and caste, have been of great influence in economic history. Also influential, as we shall see, has been the "household"—the manor, the plantation, the estate, and the dynasty. But increasingly a distinction is made between "business" and the affectional and generational bonds that hold people of a common "gene pool" together as a family. In modern economies, an enterprise that is founded by a family is increasingly conducted in "incorporated" organizations that include people outside the family and exclude members of it. The family budget and the business budget are differentiated. Nepotism is considered bad business (although marrying the boss or the boss's daughter is a time-honored way of joining the company). Even the "mom and pop shop" and the family farm increasingly depend on corporate suppliers or marketers, if the latter do not entirely take over local outlets or producers. Some children may take over their parents' independent business for a generation or two, but their sisters and brothers and their children work elsewhere.

Another possibility is the "cartel," which may appear among workers in the form of "guilds," or among owners of enterprises in the form of "combines." In either case, groups try to gain a monopoly over some essential product, skill, or service. These may have a highly potent short-term effect, but they seldom last. Guilds soon begin to break down as guilds. Some sell their interests to others, who become the new managers of the guild corporations. That has been the pattern of every modern "worker-owner" experiment that has attempted to revive the older guild ideal. Similarly, cartels break down in complex economies because they cannot control everything, and political and technological forces as well as competing economic forces mobilize sooner or later to overcome their efforts. The most dramatic modern example of this, OPEC, is a case in point.

At times religious organizations have been a major means of economic organization. Temples were the first banks; paper money as a means of rational exchange of value was invented by priests; and churches, temples, mosques, monasteries, and communal sects have on occasion come to possess vast resources decisive for whole regions. In times past, religious authority controlled irrigation systems for production, trade routes for exchange and distribution, or market sites. But essentially religion is not about these things any more than it is about political power. It may be necessary to civilization that religion provide authoritative guidance to the morality of both politics and economics, but when its purpose becomes governed by economic values, something intrinsic to religion is lost. Core aspects of every great religion always accent sacrifice, not gain; obedience, not control; sharing, not producing. Reformers among the world's religions protest the commercialization of religion from the inside, while peasants, business leaders, and rulers rebel against organized religion from the outside (and expropriate its assets) when it becomes preoccupied with possessions. Organized religion makes a poor basis for economic life. Its heart cannot be in such activity.

The fifth possible organizational center for economic activity is the market. It is a social center, however, only in an indirect way. It does not produce; it only facilitates exchange. The market is less an independent social center than an arena of economic interaction governed by a set of conventions whereby representatives of the other centers of economic activity exchange goods, services, and claims to them or promises about them. These interactions and conventions allow parties to exchange assets and to assess whether they have gained or lost in the process. In simple societies, markets are episodic; in complex societies, they are continuous. No complex society can exist without markets, although they can be, within limits, politically controlled. The more they are politically controlled, the more goods and services appear on the black market. That fact reflects the rather odd reality that a market on the one hand has its own logic, and on the other hand is quite dependent on conditions outside itself. A market can exist only when something is produced for which there is a demand, when there is a relatively stable political environment, and when people have a degree of freedom to make decisions. Since politics cannot totally control human freedom, people will always exchange goods and services for gain, creating a market in every environment. Where markets are most expansive, the people and the political authorities manifest a confidence in the economic viability of the social system as a whole.

No modern economy, however, manifests complete confidence in the market. A large number of products for which there seems to be a demand — from drugs to prostitution to votes to classified research to privileged information — are controlled. They may not be bought and sold on the market. Similarly, labor may be bought, but only under regulated conditions. Indeed, it is perhaps only because the market is politically and legally regulated that it works in predictable enough ways for people to have confidence in it.

The sixth and seventh possible centers for economic activity are those that dominate public debate today: the state and the corporation. The former entails more direct control over individuals, family businesses, religion, and the market, and the other allows more freedom for them while also pressing them toward corporate modes of organization. It may have looked to some, for nearly seven decades of this century, that "state capitalism" of either the socialist or the fascist variety was to be the instrument of modernization, the wave of the future. The government was to be the center of capitalization, the planner of production and distribution, and the agent to rationalize economic activity against the vested interests of individuals, leading families (or dominant clans, tribes, and castes), monopolistic guilds, organized religion, the independent corporations, and the market. And in some places around the world this vision of the future continues to gain ground. But wherever it is successful, institutions established for economic production and distribution are removed from direct state control and granted a relative autonomy to make decisions about the manufacture, transportation, and marketing of goods and the provision of services. The results look more like "corporations" than socialist or fascist governments advertise. Further, it has been decided on the basis of both profound moral reflection and world wars that if "state capitalism" is to going to persist, socialist forms are more benign than fascist forms. The reason is that the socialist forms attempt to deal with economic questions in a rational way and with a commitment to those on the lower end of the economic scale, whereas fascist forms celebrate irrationality and allow the systemic exploitation of the poor by supporting and getting support from elite, officially licensed cartels. But today even the socialist forms of state capitalism seem capable of fulfilling planned economic goals only by allowing families, some "guilds," *and* various "departments" and industries to function more and more as if they were independent corporations interacting in markets.

The great theological giants of previous generations might well have been disappointed at this. Shailer Mathews, Walter Rauschenbusch, Karl Barth, Reinhold Niebuhr, Paul Tillich, Martin Luther King, Jr. — all had, in their own ways, socialist inclinations. So also have the liberationists today. And most of the pastors who have come under these influences have a vision of social justice and righteousness somewhat tinged by socialism, however harshly critical of dogmatic Marxism, Leninism, and Communism they tend to be. Thus we have an apparent discrepancy between dimensions of our recent theological heritage and the decisive modern institutions of production, distribution, and consumption, to which more and more of the world seems committed.

THE CORPORATION: IN NEED OF
THEOLOGICAL ASSESSMENT

The continued growth of the influence of the corporation in modern life seems, in the short term, to be confirmed by the fact that in recent years the democratic socialist nations in Europe have all moved steadily away from state capitalist (socialist or Fascist) tendencies. They have denationalized industry and strengthened the corporations in a process called "privatization." This pattern is being followed in Africa, where various attempts at "African socialism" have brought economic disaster. And this pattern is present in the rising stars of Asia—notably Japan and now China—countries in which it is grafted onto other religiocultural traditions. The United States and Canada now have more intercorporate trade with Asia than with Europe, a phenomenon shifting the center of commercial life from the Atlantic community to an emerging and vigorously capitalist Pacific community of nations. And despite the current vigor of liberation theology in Latin America, the larger nations of that region are also turning to a renewal of democratic patterns with increased roles for corporations, while socialist efforts elsewhere end only in the sharing of poverty.

Yet very few efforts have been made to deal with the corporation in religious or theological terms. Modern public theology has addressed economic questions in some detail—particularly in regard to duties of equity in distribution. We know that we have a spiritual and moral obligation to care for poor people, and to act politically to see that oppressed groups are given a decent chance in economic life. But we have given very little theological attention to the decisive center of production: the corporation. Modern spiritualities have stressed the importance of identifying with the poor and reading the gospel through their eyes. But theologians have seldom thought about one of the most influential social institutions of modern economies, one now sweeping the world.

One of the reasons why our recent theological forebears may have failed to grasp the importance of the corporation is that they were forced to confront great political challenges in this century. Because they faced the threats of Fascism and Communism, politics was a major preoccupation. These theological leaders gave powerful political witness for which we should continue to be grateful. They articulated the theological underpinnings for pluralistic political democracies under constitutional law that protected the civil rights of minorities. They and their followers spread the spirituality of these political concerns among the people. Their thought connected with the biblical and traditional resources of faith, was reasonable in the face of madness, and was sensitive to the experience of the people. But their economic views were not so well developed or so widely infused into modernity.

Some of these concerns have been taken up in a new way by the Roman Catholic bishops of the United States and Canada. The one group is closer to "democratic capitalism," the other to "democratic socialism." Both have attempted to set forth public theological perspectives in interaction with motifs from liberation theology to produce something of a new spirituality that is at once prophetic and priestly. They recover and rearticulate biblical and ethical norms for economic life. They call for policies that defend human rights, that ensure full employment, that demand movement toward more equitable distribution of goods and services, and that defend the poor against exploitation. They warn against private greed and gluttony, and they acknowledge the role of government in economic life. They also call for programs to enhance international economic responsibility.[2]

The motifs of these recent Catholic efforts parallel motifs present in the efforts of modern Protestant heirs of the Social Gospel.[3] And for these contributions we can be grateful. On these points of distribution and consumption, they direct our attention to the kind of spirituality that we need to cultivate among the people — a spirituality quite in line with the deepest and broadest principles of Christian authority from Scripture, Tradition, Reason, and Experience, and quite in agreement with the attempts to develop a "Christian sociology" during the past century. It is surely authentic Christian witness.

But — and this is the reason for the focus of this chapter — these efforts do not significantly address the more difficult problem of the corporation as the center of production. Again and again in these various documents and in the attitudes and programs that

2. See the National Conference of Catholic Bishops, *Pastoral Letter on the Economy;* and the Canadian Conference of Catholic Bishops, *Economic Justice for All.*

3. See, for example, R. K. Taylor, *Economics and the Gospel* (Philadelphia: United Church Press, 1973); J. P. Wogaman, *The Great Economic Debate: An Ethical Analysis* (Philadelphia: Westminster Press, 1982); Prentiss Pemberton and Daniel Finn, *Toward a Christian Economic Ethic* (Minneapolis: Winston Press, 1985); and Douglas John Hall, *Imaging God: Dominion as Stewardship* (Grand Rapids: Eerdmans, 1986).

they attempt to engender, it is simply presumed that modern technological economies have solved the problem of production, and that the only remaining problems are the inequities of distribution. The inequities, it is often held, are compounded by the fact that today we are caught up in a demonic consumerism into which we are driven by corporations' seductive manipulation of desire.

Here I must introduce a personal note. In the past I have believed these things. I have preached and taught just these charges. It is commitments such as these that have driven me, during the last fifteen years, to spend every study leave and sabbatical plus several summers either in Third World countries or in the socialist lands of eastern Europe, where significantly different modes of production are in operation. I found that I was substantially in error. Not only do traditional and socialistic economic systems enhance those social forces that inhibit the development of democracy, but in them problems of maldistribution and rampant consumerism are at least as dramatic, if not more striking, than they are in the West. When either traditional or state-capitalist economies are examined, it appears that the evils of inequitable distribution and gluttonous consumerism are not rooted only in the modern Western structures of production.

There are perhaps deeper reasons for the fact that modern theology has not developed a perspective pertinent to production in corporations. Much of the protest against them, while it sounds "progressive," may be quite reactionary. It may be governed by a romantic memory of a dead past. After all, during all the biblical periods, agriculture was the primary mode of production, inducing an organic view of reality. Agriculture bonds people to the land, to the cycles of nature, and to what the ancient Greeks called *oikos,* the householder community. And as we have already noted, *oikos* is the root word for both economics and ecumenics. In that context, as Douglas Meeks shows in his forthcoming book, *God the Economist,* the problems of distribution were the central ones. Every individual's consumption was limited; everyone was expected to play a fixed role in production according to age, sex, and marital status; and it was assumed that God had already given in creation all that was needful for abundant life if everyone only followed the given order of things.

Further, the capacities for production and consumption were limited by two of the decisive structures of society that always influence economics: technology and politics. Technical capacity was limited to relatively mild interventions in the ecological order.

(Still, the herding of cattle, sheep, and goats brought overgrazing, and cutting down stands of trees to get firewood and lumber and to clear land for planting resulted in enduring erosion. The effects of these ancient economic patterns still plague the Middle East, and the patterns are being replicated in many lands today with effects more devastating than industrial pollution, as we have recently seen in North Africa.) And political governance depended on *oikos*-centered production for its resources. Indeed, the great political powers were themselves households writ large.

Similar patterns were dominant in most of the world's religions and in the church's history. Indeed, for centuries the church held that only productivity from the land was morally proper. Trade and commerce and finance were morally suspect, in part because it was held that only God's creation could be fecund.[4] Only nature could produce that which was necessary and proper for the maintenance of the human *oikos*. "Business" was at best a necessary evil that took wealth outside the *oikos* where it belonged by skimming off "surpluses" from yeoman families for private gain. It was an activity to be conducted only by wandering peddlers, greedy money-changers, and other alien or alienated peoples divorced from the proper ties of home and family. Any turn to "business" was surely a manifestation of avarice, a departure from nature and spirituality. Indeed, truly spiritual people who did not live in an *oikos* were to take vows of poverty and chastity in a "religious household" of perfect sharing, eschewing altogether the values of productivity and exchange for gain. In short, production and commerce were morally and spiritually proper only when controlled by familial or monastic patterns of distribution and supportive of traditional authority.

I have dwelt on these matters at some length — although still all too simply and briefly — because it is often held that the Christian and Western traditions concerning economics have produced a radical individualism in contrast to more communally oriented traditions elsewhere in the world. It needs to be stressed that this is only a deceptive half-truth. The basic traditions of the West do have a high regard for the human person as the seat of the God's image, as a sinner whose personal response to God's grace is decisive for redemption, and as an agent of God's will in the world. But that personal accent is always made in the context of com-

---

4. See Benjamin Nelson, *The Idea of Usury* (Princeton: Princeton University Press, 1949).

munity. The much more decisive question for modern economic life is *which* community is to be the primary locus of production, distribution, and consumption. Thus the reason for rehearsing these neglected but important motifs out of our past is that the overwhelming majority report from history gives this answer: *household,* and, in fact, all that "household" has entailed in terms of stereotypical roles of males and females, parents and children, inheritance laws, and the moral inferiority of business. This accent has been reinforced by a parallel accent on political life designed to reinforce and support the accent on the family.

Yet something happened between the earlier days of agrarian *oikos* and contemporary economies, something that produced a society quite different from these accents — something that altered structures of production and exchange especially. And that something was the development of corporations distinct from both *oikos* and the established patterns of traditional political control. To be sure, the influences of household and regime did not disappear from economic life, but they began to play subsidiary functions. Family increasingly became the arena of consumption but not of production. Portions of the structures of distribution became relegated to governmental control — especially aspects of redistribution through taxation that built the infrastructure of roads, bridges, schools, hospitals, sanitation facilities, and, more recently, welfare. These are the modern applications of very ancient theologically grounded principles about sharing in the *oikos,* supported by regime.

But more striking than all of these, and what divide modern economic systems from those of the past, are three things: technology, which will be the focus of the next chapter; the rise of the professions, which we will take up thereafter; and the formation of the business corporation, which is the question now before us. Indeed, the corporation is the modern social center of technology and of the professions. And what is remarkable about the corporation is that it has become the fundamental locus of productivity and commerce on which modern economies depend. Most contemporary pastors and theologians simply do not know what to think about that, and their witness on economic matters is not believed by the laity who have accepted the corporation as the proper basis of economic life.

DEFINING THE CORPORATION

Where did the corporation come from? What are its foundations? Where is it going? How shall we assess it morally? Is there any spirituality connected with it that can be approved, or is it simply the organized unleashing of the greed that the majority report of the church's traditions always suspected to be present in nonagricultural production, trade, commerce, and finance?

We know that there are two dead-end answers to these questions. One comes from the fundamentalist emphasis on individualistic salvation, the religious parallel to laissez-faire capitalism. It is a matter of no small irony that today's most celebrated opponents of "secular humanism" are frequently the perpetrators of one of the most virulent forms of ideological secular humanism when it comes to economic life. They have uncritically accepted the utilitarian, Enlightenment understandings of individualistic economics, the modern heirs of which — Ludwig von Mises, Friedrich Hayek, and Ayn Rand, among others — would be contemptuous of fundamentalist religion, and of the idea that religion should influence economics. These fundamentalists obscure the ways in which this ideological construct in fact works out psychologically, legally, and sociologically. In their zeal to support "individual" economic and religious responsibility, they idolize the family as the locus for the accumulation and control of wealth. It is no accident that fundamentalists who baptize this form of secular humanism have a weak ecclesiology and a preference for any political regime that will protect the traditional family and capitalist values.

The other dead-end answer is offered by liberationism when it consciously or preconsciously adopts anticorporate views because of its attraction to Marxist modes of social analysis. This perspective sees the development of corporations as the result of the ascendency of an essentially alienated yet controlling class over a dispossessed class, a problem that requires solution by revolutionary action and the political control of all means of production. Such an orientation, if the revolution succeeds, turns the whole society into a single corporation managed by the revolutionary party. Those who control the guns also control the factories; those who control the army also control the food. Each "enterprise" becomes a department of state and is required to make economic decisions on the basis of the approved political ideology. Neither of these options considers it possible to accept the moral or spiritual legitimacy of the corporation, to see it as a viable social institution.

Ought we then turn to "business" to find ways of understanding the corporation? We will find that doing so is not very helpful. Many business leaders have not focused on the basic social, historical, and spiritual foundations of their own institutions and activities. Most simply presume a social, historical, and spiritual context in which corporate patterns of doing business appear to be settled, and they proceed to carry out — with as much dispatch, energy, efficiency, and profitability as they can muster — the tasks at hand. Like the physicist who takes no interest in the structure of the university or the surgeon who gives little attention to the question of what makes a hospital run, many in business are blind to the character of the structures in which they live and move and have their being. Several years ago a team of scholars at Harvard Business School inquired into the worldviews of American business leaders. The still unsurpassed result, *The American Business Creed,* demonstrated that most business leaders hold an outmoded ideological view of their sphere of expertise that does not correspond with what they do every day or with the kinds of social interactions that actually dominate their lives.

Unfortunately, it is also not possible to turn to many contemporary economists on this matter. Most seem to be so preoccupied with developing econometric models of how specific functions work that they ignore larger questions of political economy. Yet those concerned with the clarification of a public theology for political economy cannot let the matter rest. Nor should we simply reduplicate what business leaders or economists do. We want to assess the moral viability of the contexts they presume, the spiritual and moral character of the great mechanisms of productivity that they staff. Above all, we want to know whether corporations must remain the enemy of the most spiritually, ethically, and socially concerned people, as sometimes now seems to be the case.

Where then shall we turn and what questions shall we pose if we want to understand production and the social forms that govern it? I think that we will have to inquire more deeply into the social and religious history behind the modern business corporation. It is the product, empirically, of a minority tradition in the history of religion and society. This minority tradition induced a particular kind of spirituality and a particular social orientation to the world that have roots in the history of the church and that have produced a "non-natural" form of organization with its own internal logic that is today both triumphant and suspect.

The first thing to say about the business corporation is that it is a *persona ficta,* an artifact with its own internal "spirit" or "character" and with legal standing as an agent, an actor, in human affairs. Owners, managers, and workers come and go in the corporation, but the corporation lives on. It can sue and be sued, issue contracts, hold, buy, or sell property, migrate from country to country, "get married" in mergers, produce offspring in the form of subsidiaries, be granted citizenship in other lands, grow and expand, or shrink and be executed by being dissolved. The corporation may be owned by individuals, families, other corporations, governments, labor unions, or church pension funds. It may be managed by males or females, blacks or whites, old or young, Hindus or Muslims, Jews or atheists. Workers may spend forty years in its employ, or there may be an employee turnover every five years. All this will make no essential difference regarding what it does or does not do. The corporation, for all its massive influence, is founded on a very narrow base. It is a community of persons designed for efficient production that must base every decision on the question of whether or not it can continue to produce. This is determined by whether or not it is likely to reap a legal profit that will perpetuate its existence. If it does not make a profit, or if it does so by illegal means, its managers will be fired, its owners will sell their interest in it, and it can be taken into receivership for either revitalization or dissolution. If it does make a profit, it is in principle immortal.

How did such a thing come about? The story is too complex to recount in full here, but clues can be found in the work of nineteenth-century legal historians,[5] by leading social theorists early in this century,[6] and in several newer works.[7] The roots of the phenomenon are decidedly religious, in spite of the fact that much of traditional religion resisted — and still resists — the corporation.

THE RELIGIOUS ROOTS OF THE CORPORATION

The early church established the household of faith, an *oikoumene,* a spiritual network of persons who were one in Christ who also formed a social-institutional center independent of both the tradi-

---

5. See H. S. Maine, *Ancient Law* (Oxford: Oxford University Press, 1888); and Otto Gierke, *Natural Law and the Theory of Society* (Boston: Beacon Press, 1957).

6. See G. P. Davis, *The Corporation* (New York: Harper, 1908); and Max Weber, *Economy and Society: An Outline of Interpretive Sociology,* 3 vols., ed. Guenther Roth and Claus Wittich, trans. E. Fischoff et al. (Totowa, N.J.: Bedminster Press, 1968).

7. See Harold Berman, *Law and Revolution: The Formation of the Western Legal Tradition* (Cambridge: Harvard University Press, 1983); and Brian Tierney, *The Crisis of Church and State, 1050-1300* (New York: The Free Press, 1964).

tional *oikos* and the regime. In doing so, the church established in practice, and later in law, the notion that it was possible to form collective identities that were "non-natural" in origin and that were dedicated to the transformation of every aspect of life. At first, as we see in the Book of Acts, the church established a community only of consumption, not of production. Yet this set the precedent for disciplined use of economic resources by an organized group independent of familial or imperial control.

Throughout its early period, Christianity seems to have been most appealing precisely to those marginal groups that were not engaged in landholding, in agricultural production, or in the service of the rulers. It seems to have been quite attractive to urban workers — not only urban slaves but artisans, traders, tent-makers, and the like. In brief, Christianity has been linked from its inception to urbanized peoples involved in producing and trading. Those tied to the land and its duties of *oikos* were called pagans; those who gave primary loyalty to regime were called idolaters. Against these, the church developed its own corporate structures and disciplines that were to be the prototypes of later corporate structures of many kinds.

Much later, as the medieval cities developed, stimulated in part by the new methods of production introduced into northern Europe by the monastic missionaries, a series of legal provisions established the city itself as a corporation. Like the church, it was also independent of *oikos* and regime. In addition, hospitals, schools, and other charitable corporations were formed on the analogy of the church and its orders.

At the hands of Protestant lawyers, during the period when protodemocratic political institutions were also being formed, this long tradition was extended by the formation of the limited-liability corporation, developed specifically for commercial purposes. This made it possible for people to invest in companies without risking personal, familial, or political capital distinct from that which was invested. Imbued with the Protestant work ethic, a dedication to "covenantal relationships," an inclination to bring all aspects of life under disciplined rational control, a drive toward the democratization of piety, politics, and social relationships of all kinds, and a radicalization of the sense of vocation, the limited-liability corporation developed the concept of "trustee" and invented a new social form for stewardship. The patterns consequently developed contributed to and grew with the Industrial Revolution as it introduced modern technologies of production and new occupational possibilities on a massive scale. The ethos of the corporation, which still bears the marks of this history in its deepest fabric, continues to imbue all those working in the corporation with values rooted in this history: common economic action demands a work ethic, a set of values separate from familial and political control, a discipline guided by rational control, at least a sense of "profession," and a stewardship of wealth that is not one's own. Workers and managers in modern corporations continue to be drawn into an ethos wherein these moral and spiritual presuppositions are seen as "natural," although the overt theological foundations have largely been replaced by utilitarian and contractual understandings of human relationships, and mammon has become, for many, the reigning deity.

Today, in the United States, where these developments are, if anything, more prevalent than anywhere else in the world, approximately thirteen percent of the population (and of the gross national product) is related to political and military matters, about seventeen percent of the work force is employed in nonprofit organizations, and only about three percent of the population is engaged in agriculture and family farming. All other production is in the hands of the corporations, and the profits derived make possible churches, schools, hospitals, the arts, welfare services, and various research institutes. Corporations have created more wealth than most of humankind can imagine, and they seem likely to do so in the foreseeable future. What was once rooted in *oikos* and transformed by *oikoumene* has become a corporate economy — now significantly independent not only of *oikos* and *polis* but of *oikoumene* as well.

In this context it is important to ask what "profit" is. In one sense that is what drives the corporation, and it is dedication to profit that occasions the most frequent critique of the idea that there is some viable spirituality in corporate life. Profit has a very technical and precise meaning, and organizing for it is not to be equated too quickly or too simply with either the motivation of greed or the impulse to acquisition. Max Weber already pointed that out in 1918, although theologians more than anyone else seem to have missed the point. Greed and the impulse to acquisition — indeed, the "pursuit of gain, of money, of the greatest possible amount of money" — in themselves have nothing to do with what is distinctive to the modern corporation's "profit."

> This impulse existed and has existed among waiters, physicians . . . , artists, prostitutes, dishonest officials, soldiers, nobles, crusaders, gamblers, and beggars. One may say that it has been common to all sorts and conditions of men at all times and in all countries of the earth. . . . It should be taught in the kindergarten of cultural history that this naive idea of . . . capitalism must be given up once and for all.[8]

This is so because profit involves a difference between assets and liabilities as indicated by a balance sheet figure, itself derived from the formally calculated pluses over minuses after an analytical assessment has been made on standardized principles. Profit is the estimated claim on wealth that can be used as capital for new efforts to create wealth. It is most frequently associated with the *constraint* of greed, of the impulse to acquire by chance, adventure, or expropriation and to consume. Further, profit can be understood only in the context of ongoing institutions such as corporations and exchange marts. Individuals, families, schools, hospitals, pirates, a tribe that discovers oil on its property, or a church that is the beneficiary of a will may have gains of which they want more or expenses of which they want fewer, but they do not have profits unless they are organized as corporations that produce goods and services and have rationally calculated costs and claims on income. And it is precisely such calculations that break the power of non-economic values over economic decision-making. In accounting procedures, profits serve to indicate whether previous calculations have been correct, whether economic activity has been conducted with relative efficiency and disciplined control, and whether the gain has been acquired irrespective of any special political, familial, or cultural influence that might interfere with economic calculation. This understanding of profit applies to socialist as well as capitalist economies, although in socialist economies the state calculates, collects, and deploys profits. State capitalism turns the entire nation-state into a single corporation with government as the manager of both production and markets.

Today there is another form of corporate capitalism that reigns in some regions. In the East and many developing lands, old familial networks have been incorporated into a kind of "shogunate" corporatism that is highly paternalistic, patriarchal, hierarchical, and wedded by family connections to those who control govern-

---

8. Weber, *The Protestant Ethic and the Spirit of Capitalism,* in *From Max Weber,* ed. Gerth and Mills (Oxford: Oxford University Press, 1947), p. 17.

ment. In India, subcastes have become corporations. And in Latin America, Indonesia, and the Philippines, military elites closely tied to the government are awarded control over corporations to form a kind of "crony capitalism." In these settings, the utilitarian, contract-based corporations exported from the West have little historic connection with the theological-ethical traditions that I outlined earlier. They have no history of breaking with the power of traditional familial and political institutions; instead, they reinforce them. Further, there seldom exists a legacy of law, a societal ethos, or genuine competition to control their behavior. Corporations thus are very different in the Third World than they are in the corporate capitalist West, or under state capitalism, and they are intensely resisted for good reasons.

At present there are no institutions at the international level that can control these institutions except other corporations that do a better job of producing at a lower price. And we must acknowledge that the drive to capture markets has led all forms of modern corporate production to engage political forces in imperialistic ways. In fact, in developing countries, most of the Western-based, transnational corporations betray the very foundations of what I have been attempting to set forth. More often than not, such corporations do not maintain the relative independence from either the leading households or the political regime that they attempt to maintain at home. They form alliances (or subsidiaries) with elite households and with military-political authorities to gain monopolistic controls, and they function as cartels to preserve the economic control of landed aristocracy over peasantry, which has been the pattern for centuries. They incline toward the fascist form of state capitalism, and they are properly opposed by both democratic capitalism and all democratic socialism as well as by every serious public theology. The obvious difficulties in which Third World countries currently find themselves are in part due to the failure of Western-based corporations to export their own fundamental assumptions and to equip the peoples to undertake corporate development, and the making of profits, on their own.

Such failures inhibit the capacity of concerned Western Christians to enhance things beyond productivity in these lands — namely, human rights and the prospects for democracy. Even in the rising economies of Asia, transnational corporate involvements have not brought about demonstrable respect for human rights or viable democracy, although they have brought about technological transformations and increased professionalization, the consequences of which are not yet clear. It could be that human rights, democracy, technology, professional development, and corporate productivity are among the things (besides Christianity) that the West has to offer the world, and that development of these things in modernizing cultures is being inhibited by contemporary corporate policies that ally corporations too closely with political authority and indigenous feudal elites, and that do not attend to the deeper principles on which corporate activities are grounded.

REFORMING THE SPIRITUALITY OF THE CORPORATION

If the discussion of these matters thus far can serve as a rough outline of social and spiritual factors that we must deal with in a responsible stewardship of modern political economies, and if we are fundamentally committed to a public theology that hopes to make the Word enfleshed in this kind of world, what shall the *oikoumene* now offer to corporate life?

We will have to make some very fundamental and fateful decisions before we proceed very far. One involves answering a basic question: Which form of corporative organization do we want to champion? There are only three major choices institutionally. Shall we call for state-engineered corporative life, which is the socialist route? Shall we foster an *oikos*-based corporative model, which dominates the Third World? Or shall we endorse the model of the independent corporation, an endorsement implicit in the direction the West has taken in the past? The question could be put another way: Who do we want to have calculating and making the profits and thus controlling capitalization — governments, elite families, or stockholders? I do not think it will do for ecumenical leadership to continue to duck this issue by continuing to ignore the questions of production and concentrating only on distribution, however important it is to maintain ethical witness on that front.

I think that we had better choose the model of the independent corporation (although in some situations the state-socialist model may have to be employed temporarily to remove elite families from their present positions of economic exploitation). We should do so because, in the long run, it is the system most inclined to support and sustain the prospects for human rights, democratic participation in political life, and the reduction of feudal, patriarchal, and caste structure in family life. Of course, we must beware here, because making such a choice can easily be seen as simply a sanctification of Yankee corporate capitalism and a conscious or preconscious attempt to wrap the American way of life in the Christian flag and drape it around the world. These I do not intend, and hence any move in the direction I suggest must be coupled with simultaneous prophetic judgment against and pastoral reformation of many current corporate policies.

Unlike many arguments today, the argument in these pages is not based on a dialectical reading of history. But if it were, part of what is suggested here could be understood in different terms than those used here. It could be said that *oikos*-based feudalism has produced and still tends to produce its antithesis, capitalistic individualism; and that the synthesis, "robber barons," produces its antithesis of state capitalism. That has brought us the socialisms and fascisms of the twentieth century, against which the reactionary forces of individualistic and state capitalism are presently arrayed. We do not yet have a viable antithesis to this present state of affairs except the ideal of social democracy borne by the ecumenical church, which must, without extensive politcal, economic, or technological power, develop a new spirituality, based on a public theology, to transform the materialist and reductionist preoccupation of all present economic forms and ideologies. This is possible because already within the modern corporation are residual ecclesiological elements wherein spiritual matters are intrinsically related to social ones, and therefore are potentially related to new patterns of material and organizational embodiment.

In order to carry out prophetic judgment against and reformation of corporations, we will have to make a second decision. Do we think that corporations have any real or potential spiritual foundations? If they do not, we can have no transformative communication base with them. We would have to see them only as mechanisms, as humanly populated machines that could be constructed or deconstructed, that break down and can be repaired, but that could not in principle be reformed by any spiritual or moral transformation.

This question is not new, although it is neglected. A generation ago, F. W. Maitland and Ernest Barker, among others, researched the question of whether institutions have souls.[9] On the whole, they argued, it cannot be held that institutions will, like people, stand before the gates of heaven. Institutions can neither

---

9. See Maitland's introduction to Otto Gierke's *Political Theories of the Middle Ages* (Boston: Beacon Press, 1959), and Barker's introduction to Gierke's *Natural Law and the Theory of Society*.

go to heaven nor suffer in hell. Yet that does not mean that corporations cannot have a character, even a certain esprit de corps that can be assessed on moral and spiritual grounds. It is quite possible that these *personae fictae,* which are more *ficta* than *persona,* have an inner quality that can be reformed and renewed.

After all, it is not so farfetched to hold that corporations have some kind of spirit or character. They are not, in fundamental ways, different from universities, orchestras, or athletic clubs, which do seem to have distinctive spirits and characters. Who does not know of someone who, when job-hunting, compares the characters of the firms involved, speaking easily about the moral "tone," the humane fabric of human relationships, the sense of purpose and professional excellence, the responsible attitudes toward employees? And is it not odd that clergy who rage against corporations and the profit motive rejoice when young women and men in their congregations join a "quality" company? In a special issue of *Word and World* (Spring 1984), a number of authors speak about the kinds of moral and spiritual engagement, stimulation, stretching beyond oneself, loyalty, and intensity that come from corporate participation, especially on the part of the baby-boom generation and the blacks and the women who have subsequently been most critical of male-dominated corporate capitalism. How do we account for the fact that they seem to find liberation in the disciplined work ethic and the quest for profits when they work in first-rate corporations? And do we not find among the most sensitive of the lay leaders in our churches those who can neither tolerate nor reform the inner quality of life in a particular corporation when its inner character is distorted or absent, and who change positions or simply quit, even when it involves a considerable reduction in income? Is it not so that workers and managers in "quality" unions and corporations sometimes have the same kinds of characterological and spiritual-communal experiences that pastors have in working with the best churches?

The problem still remains. What theological resources will we bring to bear on these facts of public life today, and what forms of spirituality ought we to attempt to cultivate for corporate life? To be sure, many argue that corporate life is inevitably spiritually vacuous, that corporations today are alienating and dehumanizing, and that a commercial enterprise surely cannot have any soul, any spirituality, for it is based, as it must be, on the making of a profit, the impersonality of the market, the mechanism of engineered needs, and finally the worship of mammon. And yet that judgment does not seem to be faithful either to the deeper history of the modern corporation (as it derived from ecclesiological, free-city, and charity-organization precedents) or to the human experience that people in our churches have in corporations.

Let us not be smug about this. Let us not uncritically celebrate the corporation today when in fact many features of corporate life produce items of little lasting value, distribute them inequitably, consume inordinate quantities of the world's nonrenewable resources, and cooperate with the most exploitative forces present in other lands. And let us not forget the horror stories of discrimination, pettiness, meanness, and the rat race told by executives and laborers alike. Our purpose is simply to overcome a blind spot in modern theology and ethics, one that can prevent us from even grappling with the nature and character of the corporation as a potentially moral and spiritual reality. I simply want to stress that there may be a core in the midst of corporate life that has become vacuous or can become demonic but that may also be filled and transformed by a theologically vertibrate spirituality.

If this is so, what resources from our theological tradition shall we bring to bear on the reformation of the spirituality of production as it appears in the modern corporation? Let me close this chapter by listing five motifs from the governing themes of a public theology (from Chapter Two) that might become the counterpoints of preaching and teaching, pastoral care, and the development of a stewardly leadership able to carry their commitments and ministries into the world of the productive corporation:

1. Vocation. From the calling of Abraham and Moses to the calling of the prophets and disciples, through the various refinements in the history of the tradition, the notion that each person was put in the world by God to serve some particular purpose and is called to serve the whole of humanity in the economy of God is a profound and penetrating insight. A vocation is not simply a job or an occupation. It comes from God and may require sacrificial suffering, discipleship, and *kenosis*. The concept has its most important application in regard to personal life, but it has social dimensions as well. Further, every institution has *its* particular vocation. Schools are to seek the truth and understanding; hospitals are devoted to healing and the care of the sick; symphonies are meant for making music. Is it possible that corporations as cooperative endeavors, as well as the people in them, have a vocation from God to do what they do? Surely this means that they must contribute to the material well-being of the human community with

the particular skills and products they offer — plumbing supply, meat-packing, energy resources, or whatever — and that they must do so in a way that makes a profit.

If this is possible, common corporate vocations must be carried out under the watchful eye of the living God with no less diligence than our personal quests for vocational fulfillment. A vocation under God is proactive — not merely reactive. Not only does it minister to those harmed by bad economic policy or corporate decisions; it steels the soul for economic initiative and engenders a willingness to take moral risks. Were the sense of vocation to be reborn in modern corporations among stockholders, management, and labor, the shape of corporate economies might change.

To accent such matters is the responsibility of clergy and theologians. Who in government, in labor unions, in business schools or economic departments speaks of these matters? It is *our* task, one we will have to address again, and more fully, in Chapter Nine.

2. Moral Law. In some circles today it seems quaint to speak of moral law, and many are so afraid of sounding self-righteous (as those who talk about it a great deal often do) that they avoid speaking of it. And yet the reluctance to speak clearly about fundamental principles of right and wrong allows people in corporate life to be satisfied on the one hand with mere legality, and on the other hand with whatever is strategic or efficient. This has allowed many to lose sight of the basic principles of human rights that must be met as a condition of any viable structure of economic life. Corporations, especially those in such places as South Africa and developing countries, must see to it that their activities enhance human rights. And if this is not the case, they must not be surprised if churches, workers' groups, opposition parties, and oppressed minorities form coalitions to convert them.

3. Liberation. In the West, millions of middle-class people have found their economic liberation — against the expectations of many — in the disciplined, cooperative sharing of vocations in corporations. Yet many on the underside of Western economies have not had this experience, and many more around the world are oppressed by corporations. If there is to be a remedy for this problem, it will mean that the long-range planning that every corporation now does and the intervening steps taken to carry out those plans must speak to this question: Does this project somehow contribute to the liberation of those not free in a way that draws them also into communities of economic responsibility?

4. Sin. There is something tragic in all of economic life. Every

act of production involves the destruction of some resource that has been given to humanity in creation, and every pattern of distribution entails disproportionate gain for some at the expense of others. and every act of consumption involves waste. Further, every organized center of economic activity thus far developed involves the domination of some over others. Let us never think that we humans can find our salvation in economic activity and its rewards, or in the building of one specific kind of economic order, including that centered in the corporation. Many corporations engender a kind of loyalty that borders on the totemic at best, on the idolatrous at worst. The tendencies to worship mammon are with us all, and can easily demand that the corporation become mammon's temple. Especially because the corporation can provide a kind of immortality, it can require human sacrifice on its altar. These perils are already suggested in the commandment that tells us that six days shall we labor, but that we must remember the Sabbath, to keep it holy. Our necessary efforts at production are disciplined and restrained by the constant and regular repair to the One who creates what we can never produce, distributes what no human system can apportion, and receives out of our willingness to consume less than we obviously could.

5. Covenant. In the face of our modern political economies, we must work out a covenantal structure for the corporation in ways framed by these other doctrines and in ways echoing the ecclesiological roots of the corporation. And we must attempt to structure economic influence by patterns that reflect what we have learned about political distributions of power. The future of corporate polity will surely demand the democratization of decision-making, the sharing of power, and the participation of labor in setting guidelines for corporate policy around the world.[10] And this means the pluralization of economic authority and a political, social, and ethical openness to corporate formation in underdeveloped regions of the world, which state capitalisms of the left and the right do not presently encourage.

---

10. See especially William J. Everett, "*Oikos:* Convergence in Business Ethics," *Journal of Business Ethics* 5 (1986): 313-25. See also Arthur Rich, *Mitbestimmung in der Industrie* (Zurich: Flamberg Verlag, 1973); S. T. Bruyn, *The Social Economy: People Transforming Modern Business* (New York: John Wiley & Sons, 1977); and Terry Deal and Allan Kennedy, *Corporate Cultures: The Rites and Rituals of Corporate Life* (Reading, Mass.: Addison-Wesley, 1982).

To this list one might easily add Creation. The modern corporation is — besides those things already discussed — the seat of modern technology that alters the structures of nature. It therefore has many implications for how we relate to the biophysical universe as a creation of God. But that is the topic of our next chapter.

Study Questions

Based on the view that corporations are the center of modern economic life, this chapter asks whether corporations are in any sense moral and spiritual institutions.

1. In the transition from family farm or business to modern corporate life, how has the individual's perception of meaning and of vocation been affected?

2. If religion speaks of sacrifice rather than gain, how is it that religious institutions have sometimes become very wealthy? Is this phenomenon related to issues of the separation of church and state, of church and business? How do you view the assets of the church?

3. Do you believe it is true that socialism as it is practiced always has overtones of capitalism? What principles of a public theology are related to this?

4. In economic theory, the inputs for production are defined as land, labor, capital, and management. What uses of these inputs result in "the injustice of production"? What role do they play in "the injustice of distribution"?

5. Do you agree that many theologians and church leaders are confused about economic matters and the nature of the corporation? If so, why do you think that this is the case?

6. In what ways does the fundamentalists' interest in preserving "the traditional family" and laissez-faire capitalism conflict with the teachings of Scripture that they claim to uphold?

7. Is there any parallel between the separation of corporation and family and the separation of church and state? Ought there to be?

8. In what ways does the structure of the corporation reflect the structure of the church in the economy of God? In what ways does it stand in tension with the structure of the church?

9. Is profit evil? Is the "profit motive" always rooted in greed? Is it wrong for economic institutions to be concerned with profits?

10. Have the goals of Western capitalism to produce efficiently and to get a larger and larger share of the market increased injustice in the world? Can such efforts be reconciled with a theological understanding of the corporation?

11. When liberation theologians of the "Third World" offer criticisms of capitalism and corporations, do they see the same things Westerners see? Why should people in the Western churches listen to their ideas about the relationship of religion and economics? Do we have any ideas to offer them in this area that are not "neo-colonial"?

12. Do you think that corporations have an "inner spirit" or "character"? Do you think that corporate "soul" can be reformed at home and abroad? If so, how? If not, what should we do?

13. Do you believe that Christians and the churches should, and can, undertake the stewardship of modern economic institutions? What do you expect pastors, business leaders, and workers to do in the economic area of life?

CHAPTER EIGHT

Sacrament and Technology

I thought about several possible titles for this chapter, and the one that almost triumphed was "Consciousness, Computers, and the Bomb." The reason that it was such a strong contender is that the computer and the bomb seem to be two of the most dramatic forms of modern technology that have changed our ideas about nature, society, the way humans think, and the degree to which we can intervene in nature. The phenomena to which these two terms refer reveal areas that are, like politics and the modern corporation, subject to religious influence, although our grasp of the long-term significance of the computer and the bomb is so recent that we have not yet sorted out, theologically or ethically, what we should do or what we should think about them. All that we say about modern technology, as manifest in the simultaneous computerization and nuclearization of the world, must remain tentative. Yet, if we are to develop a public theology for modern political economies as a part of our stewardship of the Word and of the world, we cannot remain silent. We have to attempt to say what can be said.

Our predecessors in the community of saints have influenced, both positively and negatively, what we now have. And we can modify the future by the quality of moral and spiritual witness that we shape now among the people. Technology is already being shaped by organized religion in some ways, although we are more conscious of the way it is influenced by political life and by that central home of modern technology, the corporation. It is also shaped by the new professions, as we will see in the next chapter. But technology is also influencing politics, economics, and the professions — including the ministry, and hence some aspects of theology and ethics.

Technology does not seem to have much to do with theology and ethics. More often it is understood to be a combination of three things: science, technique, and art. It begins in technique, in a method of doing something that applies known means to accomplish desired ends. Every civilization has at its disposal a wide variety of techniques, and a number of them are extraordinary. The accomplishments of the Aztecs, the ancient Egyptians, the Babylonians, and the cultures of Africa and Asia continue to amaze modern people. What distinguishes modern technology from the refined ancient techniques is that modern technology relates technique and science in two ways. First, science uses techniques to control experiments in order to find out what the world is and how it works. The purpose of science is to obtain reliable, valid knowledge. Second, technology uses science to measure the relative effectiveness of its methods and to identify intended and unintended real consequences that alter the world as it is given. In technology, therefore, science and technique have a mutually exploitative relationship, each using the other for its own ends. The application of science to technique means that technology applies a self-critical principle and changes its procedures if science proves that the intended results do not occur as expected or that unintended results bring unwanted consequences. Thus technology is innovative, with every innovation having to prove that it allows more rational and intentional control over that to which it is applied.

All technology requires art also. The carpenter, the fisherman, the potter, the mason, the farmer, the cook, the baker — all use techniques increasingly influenced by science. In their simpler forms we call these "crafts." We admire people who are good at their craft, and we admire well-crafted objects. In anthropological museums we find hunting, gathering, and farming implements that tell us much about both the skill and the art of the world's peoples. Technique in this form creates artifacts and requires specialized knowledge; the objects produced are shaped or decorated for beauty as well as for utility. Anyone who has an appreciation for quilts, handmade sweaters, vases, tools, or finely crafted bookcases will know what is involved. Such artifacts express human consciousness and entail human intervention in the biophysical cosmos. They represent transformations of what is given in creation. Even the techniques of organic gardening reorder what is natural, and they can be employed with more or less science and more or less art.

Modern technologies, from automobile manufacturing to rocket launching to the chicken farming of contemporary agribusiness, have a component of art as well. It is not nonsense to call a new car, a rocket launch, or a chicken farm "beautiful." Every technology potentially involves the creation of beauty. An aesthetic or cultural dimension is always intertwined with the technique and science of technology.

One of the key problems of dealing with technology and of attempting to shape it in new directions is that it does not have (as do most of the things we have talked about thus far) a peculiar institutional center of organization. Indeed, it is a remarkable feature of modern societies that much technology plays a part in virtually all social institutions. The modern kitchen is a nest of technological wonders. Church organizations, from local congregations to international bureaucracies, hum with the sounds of photocopiers, electric typewriters, and complex audiovisual equipment available on demand. And if we turn to a government bureaucracy, a hospital, or a university, technology is pervasive.

Technology is like language, to which it can be fruitfully compared. Language is an institution, but it has many specialized usages and particular employments in subcultural settings. It does not have a singular social locus. Further, like technology, it shapes and is shaped by changing social consciousness. Modern technology may be more intricately tied to the structures of meaning by which modern society exists than anything else except the symbols we invoke, the tongues we speak, and the cultural-linguistic channels in which our minds move. We are socialized into it, and by our peculiar usages of it, technology, like language, alters the whole structure of society.

In another way, too, modern technology requires art. Modern technologies require the interaction of large numbers of people in sometimes elaborate networks or teams that depend on one another, although they may not know one another and might not like one another if they did. Think, for a moment, of the human or social arts that must be involved in using two common forms of technology — reading the newspaper and telephoning a friend in another country. These examples illustrate a fact that connects this chapter with the two previous ones: each of these acts demands a relatively open political order and an intricate grid of interlocked corporate cooperation, each corporation involving thousands of people. The art required to gain the reliable cooperation of all these people demands a technology in human management that is astounding.

Every technology involves disruption of, intervention in, and human control over both the biophysical and the "natural" social worlds. After the workings of technology, neither the ecological order nor the social order is ever the same. Our environment becomes increasingly distinct from the cosmos as we found it, and an ethos begins to form. Technology involves the intentional transformation of the cosmos; it helps shape the ethos as its specific techniques develop in unique relationships to science and art. Technology in this sense was not fully anticipated by any of the ancient religions. It makes possible increasingly complex societies, and it involves the prospect of more dramatic interventions in the cosmos and the formation of a new ethos. It places new demands on consciousness.

The converse is also true: technology requires a particular consciousness. It is not only a fact that if the knowledge of the technique, the science, or the art is weak, the technology used and its product will be poor. It is also a fact that people have to believe in certain things in order to engage in technology at all. Some religious and metaphysical views inhibit the development of science and art and their application to techniques if they imply significant change. Other forms of belief invite, even prompt, the development of modern technology.

HOW BELIEF AFFECTS THE DEVELOPMENT OF TECHNOLOGY

Technology in the modern sense can occur only where a population (or a decisive segment of it) believes that nature is reliable — where it is held that there are "laws" governing its operation. Where this is not the case, the scientific investigation of nature does not develop. For example, science cannot develop where it is believed that nature is inhabited by spirits, demons, or the souls of ancestors or gods, or where it is believed that nature is entirely capricious. In such contexts, people may develop techniques to manipulate the irrational forces and to bring a modicum of order to nature, and these may involve elaborate arts, but such techniques will be intimately tied to the occult or to magic. Science can develop only where there is a fundamental notion that something reliable may be known about nature because nature is presumed to be orderly and not in itself so divine that it cannot be manipulated.

At the same time, science is used in transformative technique only when it is believed that something as it naturally appears in the biophysical or social world needs reordering because it is at least partially disordered and open to alteration, even if it is rational. Belief in the rationality of nature is a necessary but not a sufficient presupposition on which to base the kind of consciousness necessary for the emergence of technology. A world thought to consist in a closed determinism does not induce technology, even if it evokes scientistic philosophies. The world has to be thought of as both rational and open to further intentional modification by a rationality of a higher order. Some metaphysical-moral reality, some nature- and ethos-transcending actuality fundamentally more important than the order of nature or of society as naturally found, has to be taken as the primary point of reference. This actuality authorizes the human discovery of nature's rational patterns and the use of them to alter both the biophysical cosmos and the ethos. A metaphysical-moral vision is required that allows humans to "cook" nature into something that it is not originally, and to provide the model of that into which society ought to be transformed.

If a metaphysical-moral vision beyond nature is not present, humans have only two choices: to fit into the patterns of nature as they exist, or to make things according to the artful imaginings of their minds, wants, needs, and desires. The result of one is an "ontocratic" nature worship, the term Arend van Leeuwen uses in his major study of the impact of technology around the world.[1] The more popular view of this is seen in Frankenstein movies, in which terror is loosed upon the world by the human effort to construct life in non-natural ways. The result of the other choice is an anthropocentrism, which James Gustafson has recently described in his new study of the relationship of science and theology.[2] This view has a more ancient "hero": it was Prometheus who snatched fire, the symbol of technology, from the gods and gave it to humans, making humanity master over heaven and earth.

In wrestling with such matters, we should recognize that we

---

1. Van Leeuwen, *Christianity in World History* (New York: Scribner's, 1964).

2. Gustafson, *Ethics from a Theocentric Perspective.* 2 vols. (Chicago: University of Chicago Press, 1983-84).

are dealing with some of the most profound and fateful questions that have always confronted humanity. What is the character of the cosmos, and what is the relationship of human society, human consciousness, and divine reality to it? The theological question behind all issues of technology is this: Is it the case that we humans know something reliable about a metaphysical-moral reality that is beyond the rationality of nature, and beyond the artifacts of human techniques and art, yet not opposed to the notion that nature is rational? If we do, we have a basis for holding that true deity transcends — and is not simply a part of — nature, and that nature is secular and not sacred. Nature therefore may be altered because of and in accord with that higher authority by judicious use of the residual rationality of nature. Where this belief is not held, highly sophisticated patterns of technique may develop, a deep, spiritual affinity for nature may be felt, or artful methods of manipulating nature to satisfy human desires may be cultivated, but these responses are made either to integrate human life more fully into the primal, ontocratic structure of nature, or because humans, having something of a free will, want and are able to create their own worlds according to their own imaginations.

It is unlikely that technology in its modern forms would be developed or could be extended without a belief that something or some One beyond nature has authorized the reordering of nature. People have to believe that nature is not something that they must passively accept, simply tuning into its inherent rhythms and patterns, but something that can be and perhaps ought to be rearranged by conscious activity. The decisive question is whether that activity is governed by anything more than preference, imagination, and possibly immediate material interests.

Those religions that have spoken of a Creator God have already made a fateful decision at this point: they have come to the conviction that the only reality worth worshiping is one that is other than nature, distinct from nature but author of it. Thus nature has its rational order not because of its innate qualities but by virtue of the reasonability of that which made it. Such religions are in principle sympathetic and open to modern science. Further, these religions hold that nature is a subordinate reality to that which created it. Thus nature is not absolute and not the basic guide for our existence. Nature is creation, and we are to deal with the gift of creation under standards not of the creation itself but of its Creator. The Christian tradition, particularly in its Protestant forms, has reinforced this notion of the distinction between nature and creation by claiming that nature is also "fallen" and thus has to be reordered to be what it was intended to be. Conversion, transformation, and re-ordering are not only possible but morally and spiritually necessary for all things natural. This claim has tremendous implications for the kinds of consciousness that are possible. For if it is true, not only is science compatible with profound religion, but intentional technological transformation is demanded by it.

But many resist such ideas. Today, in ethics, in psychology, in sociology, and in a number of theologies (in process, empirical, ecological, and no small amount of feminist theology), there is a renewed accent on a purely immanental worldview that sees any transformation of that which is "natural"—conversion from a culture's indigenous religion to another one, transformation of traditional societies into modern ones, the development of cities where there were once fields and forests, the development of loyalties to those to whom we are not naturally related, or the restraint of "natural" feelings—as a violation of nature. In this view, modern technology is rooted in the fundamental fault of modern consciousness: we believe too much in a transcendent God and in a fallen world. Thus we have been tempted to adopt a dualism that makes us think that we have the permission, or even the mandate, to manipulate nature and to dominate it. Instead, we ought to re-encounter the natural creativities of our being, the thick tissues of organic relations, and rediscover the ontological patterns of holistic communitarian living. Many of the views promoting this emphasis oppose modern technology as being manipulative, arrogant, imperialistic, and destructive of "real" life.[3]

At the same time, other forms of ethics, psychology, social theories, and sometimes theology (existential, political, and radical) call for increased human planning of social change, and for the free and unconstrained use of human capacities to decide our own futures, name our own realities, and envision our own futures without reference to "old-fashioned" notions that we are under any "fixed," "natural," or transcendental constraints. Human creativity is the central point of reference; the idea that humans have to fit into some pregiven "natural laws" brings repression and oppression. In this view, the failures of modern technology are not to be found in the perils of the violation of ontology; they are seen as failures in

---

3. See Gibson Winter, *Liberating Creation: Foundations of Religious Social Ethics* (New York: Crossroad, 1981).

courage, imagination, and willingness to risk what might be made of the wondrous new science-based techniques.[4]

Modern civilization and modern theology are confused about these questions. Many of us shift our ground as various issues come before us. Eventually, however, we will have to make public decisions about whether or not we think it is fundamentally true to speak of a Creator God and whether or not we believe that the created order, including human nature and "natural" social arrangements, is fallen. If we think that these are valid truth claims, we can advocate them in the public domain in good conscience against both the ontocrats and the Prometheans, against both those who fear Frankenstein and those who are completely anthropocentric, recognizing that the embrace of these views will lead to further intentional transformations of the world by the use of technology. It would also mean that the primary task before us is to attempt to identify the purposes, principles, and institutions that could guide technology and restrain its possible misuses. It would allow that under certain conditions we can apply science and art to technique and intervene in the cosmos and the ethos as people called by God to be agents of the right reordering of fallen nature.

What is at stake here theologically are the questions of whether humans are authorized by God to utilize technology to intervene in the "natural" structures of the world, how much intervention is appropriate, what purposes are morally and spiritually proper to the use of technology, and what principles we ought to use in deciding what is right and wrong in such matters. How we sort out these questions theologically, ethically, and practically has implications for a good bit of the world. Let us look at the major options more closely.

A generation ago, Arend van Leeuwen argued that modern science-based technology is a product of the Judeo-Christian assumptions about the relationship of God, humanity, and the cosmos that are universally true. Today technology is changing the face of the earth and being adopted everywhere, and every culture or civilization that adopts technology is undergoing (intentionally or not) a transformation of consciousness. Indeed, van Leeuwen argues that technology is a new form of evangelism that is also building the foundations for a genuinely cosmopolitan faith. Anyone who adopts it will ultimately have to adopt the foundations on which it

---

4. See Joseph Fletcher, *Moral Responsibility: Situation Ethics at Work* (Philadelphia: Westminster Press, 1967).

rests. Technology thus functions as a kind of veiled angel who brings a fundamental change of consciousness as well as new opportunities to alter what was once regarded as fate. Any full-fledged adoption of technology will demand a new awareness of creation, the Fall of creation, and eventually the Creator of creation, who authorizes the reordering of nature in specific ways, under moral constraints, for the benefit of all humans.[5] In this view, the fascination for science and technology that is present in modern Communism is a secularized version of a godly faith, one that is providentially cracking open and undermining the ancient ontocratic civilizations of Asia and Latin America. However, the transformations that it brings will not be able to reconstruct civilization, only to destroy what must be destroyed. If reconstruction is to take place, the deeper theological assumptions, of which Communism offers only heretical forms, will have to be invoked.

It is also possible to argue, as some do today, that one tradition has indeed produced something that is universal in implication, but universal in a negative sense. This view holds that modern technology may well have been derived from Judeo-Christian presuppositions, but that it has now lost any rootage in theological considerations. It has become entirely autonomous, a new kind of fallen angel that is demonic and out of the control of humanity or God. In this view, modern technology is scientifically empowered technique that dehumanizes us by promising us mastery of the world yet inexorably further alienating us from God and moral responsibility. While it seems to bring freedom in the face of old natural necessities, it is in fact oblivious to nature's rationality, human freedom, and a Creator God. It destroys its creators in the long run. Instead of placing our confidence in technique, we need to return to absolute reliance on the free will of God, known by revelation alone. Jacques Ellul makes such an indictment in his widely known book *The Technological Society.*[6]

One of the few modern ecumenical scholars to take up these questions of technology in a sustained theological way that is neither so optimistic as van Leeuwen's nor so pessimistic as Ellul's is Roger Shinn. His book *Forced Options* ought to be required reading for pastors today. In a nuanced and readable way, he shows that the entire world is now facing certain very critical problems in the areas of water supply, land erosion, population explosion, food sup-

5. Van Leeuwen, *Christianity in World History*.
6. Ellul, *The Technological Society* (New York: Vintage Books, 1964).

ply, energy, and atomic warfare. All of these problems are exacerbated by modern technology, and none of them can be addressed without the positive use of technology. It will not help humanity one whit to believe that technology has developed its own demonic, autonomous power before which humanity is powerless, or to hold that technology is purely the manifestation of godly forces, a slightly disguised but unalterable blessing.[7]

Although van Leeuwen and Ellul each take a different direction, both represent technology too simplistically. Technology is neither so angelic as van Leeuwen claims nor so demonic as Ellul insists. Every new constellation of technology will bring with it a passel of new problems and crises, just as every employment of language simultaneously reveals and obscures meaning. The benefits and the liabilities of medical technology serve as an example. This technology has saved lives by the millions — but it is also the factor that has contributed most to the world's population crisis. The technology of transportation provides another example: its present forms allow us to visit anywhere in the world, but at the same time they threaten pollution of the planet.

THE BOMB AND THE COMPUTER: THE AMBIGUITY OF TECHNOLOGY MADE PLAIN

Nowhere is the ambiguity of technology more apparent than in two of the most dramatic creations of modern technology: the bomb and the computer. Both are products of high-tech society. Each has penetrated our consciousness and forced us to raise new questions about what kind of world we want to live in and what kind we ought to live in, even if we are able to hold the destructive potentialities of these developments in check and to find their possible constructive potentialities. We are not very far along on either of these fronts, yet the bomb in its morally scandalous function of maintaining the balance of terror and offering mutual assured destruction may yet ethically inhibit competing worlds from arrogantly forcing their own ways of life on others. It provokes the most virulent forms of the Promethean absolutizing of technology while at the same time it demands the negotiated relaxation of tensions. And yet we know in the depths of our consciousness, we see portrayed in our modern technologized arts of film and television, and

---

7. Shinn, *Forced Options: Social Decisions for the Twenty-First Century* (San Francisco: Harper & Row, 1981).

we hear from our scientists and technological reporters — from Carl Sagan, the prophet of "nuclear winter," to Jonathan Schell, the author of *Fate of the Earth* — that the balance of terror just might fail. Escalation of the nuclear arms race, not negotiated reduction of tensions, may be our destiny. We might very well be confronted with a nuclear catastrophe that would annihilate not only humanity but also every living thing on earth. This would mean the obliteration not only of the human future but also of the future of life itself in any known form. Modern technology in the form of the bomb could entail a cosmic intervention of such proportions that it would make the Holocaust look like child's play.

Gordon Kaufman, one of the outstanding theologians of our day and a Mennonite in background, reflected on this prospect in a major plenary address at the 1982 meeting of the American Academy of Religion. Later he expanded these reflections in a series of lectures he gave in England. He argues that very deeply rooted in Western religious traditions — in ancient Hebrew scriptures and throughout Christian writings — is an expectation of a final judgment of God, a consummation of history, a Day of the Lord in which destruction portends a final future. And in this tradition this expectation is always modified by hope, by a notion that the terrible moment will also bring with it the prospect of ultimate salvation: in that time God will ultimately and finally triumph over evil, wickedness, and injustice. Kaufman then asks whether a nuclear holocaust is of this order. He thinks it is not. He is sharply critical of those fundamentalists of the far right who see this prospect as the "ultimate expression of God's sovereignty over history" and argue that we must prepare for Armageddon. He is equally critical of those who simply hold that "God's providential care will surely not allow us to destroy ourselves in a nuclear holocaust."[8]

Kaufman points out that nuclear technology brings us face to face with the question of ultimate limits, a question that people have always had to face personally in terms of their own deaths and the death of loved ones, but a question that is now of such massive proportion that all the ultimate questions of faith are forced to the fore as public issues. Can we, for example, continue to believe Paul's assurance that "*nothing . . . can separate us from the love*

---

8. Kaufman's address, "Nuclear Eschatology," was printed in the March 1983 issue of *JAAR*, pp. 3-14. The series of lectures was collected in *Theology for a Nuclear Age* (Philadelphia: Westminster Press, 1985). The quotations in this paragraph are found on p. 8 of that volume.

of God in Christ Jesus our Lord"? Or does the threat of nuclear destruction nullify this promise?

It may be that Kaufman has overstressed the notion that we are in an entirely new situation where everything has to be thought through again from scratch; indeed, on many points I do not find him convincing in this regard. Yet he articulates the pastoral and public theological question forcefully: From what perspective shall we address these matters? What do we have to say about life and the death, nonbeing, emptiness, and destruction brought about by one of the key examples of modern technology?

It simply will not do to appeal to people's sense of survival. Every effort to mobilize people for peace efforts tends to flounder when mere survival is the primary point of appeal. Of course, we all want to survive, but that is not the deepest question. People want and need, at a much deeper level (of which they may not themselves be fully aware), to know something about meaning, about the meaning of life and death, about the end or purpose of it all, about how good and evil can be so mixed and mixed-up in such brilliant technology that is also our cultural fabric, our civilizational base, our consciousness. Unless we have something to say about this as a matter of public theology, we might as well remain silent, as most of us tend to do most of the time. But if we do not speak, the Prometheans or the demonizers, the technological missionaries or the Armageddonites will shape the consciousness of the people to no good end.

My own view is that we are now in a situation that will last as long as history lasts, a situation in which we will have to live with the prospect of nuclear destruction and must therefore be constantly confronted with the ultimate questions of good and evil with a new immediacy. I do not believe that we will ever again have a technological society in which nuclear destruction is not a possibility. Even if we dismantled all the present weapons and entered agreements not to construct new ones, the capacity to build them is already woven into the fabric of modernity and spreading around the world. The know-how is in the minds of scientists, in libraries, in computers, in laboratory records, and in secret time capsules of the military. This knowledge could be expunged only by brainwashing, book burning, and drastic controls on science, engineering, and technology. Only totalitarian control over thought could limit the prospects of reconstruction. And we know that, in order to get some group to undertake this purge, we would have to give it totalitarian authority, and such a group would want, first of all,

the bomb. Even if there were a nuclear exchange that did not destroy everyone and everything but simply returned us to the Stone
Age, one might expect some survivors to have knowledge about the
bomb. Barring that, the time capsules might be uncovered and their
contents deciphered. Thus the prospect of living with nuclear bombs
would return. But the deeper horror is that, whether or not we have
the know-how to build the bomb, we humans, as a fallen race, will
always *want* the know-how.

What, then, do we have to say? How is our public theology
to deal with such a terrifying prospect? I will shortly suggest that
it has something to do with the recovery of the meaning of *sacrament,* but now we must turn briefly to the second great manifestation of technology — the computer.

Joseph Weizenbaum, one of this country's leading specialists
in the technology of the artificial intelligence claimed to be produced
by computers and one of the leading scientists active in the anti-
nuclear movement, understands that the basic connections between
science, art, and technique that produced the bomb also produced
the computer. He claims that both are dangerous, the computer
because it always works in a linear, logical, and rule-governed way.
This view of reality, if it is taken too seriously, reinforces the purely
instrumental, pragmatic, and utilitarian dimensions of modern culture. If we take this as a model for what life and meaning are all
about, we derive a flattened, one-dimensional view of humanity,
the universe, and civilization. We are tempted to lose track of the
most important things of life, which are those things that "we know
but cannot tell" — things like what it means to fall in love.[9]

But others are not so sure that Weizenbaum is right. Sherry
Turkle, author of *The Second Self,* the groundbreaking new book
on computers and the human spirit, has used extensive psychological and sociological methods to investigate how people relate to
computers, and how the experience informs their consciousness
and their perceptions of reality. Turkle peppers her empirical research with reflective philosophical insights. Drawing from the re-
actions of children introduced to computers, from the reflections of
theorists, and from the responses both of the growing subculture
of "hackers" and of ordinary users, she suggests that computers
are introducing a kind of consciousness that will reform most of

9. Weizenbaum, *Computer Power and Human Reason: From Judgment to
Calculation* (San Francisco: W. H. Freeman, 1979).

the ideas we have inherited from psychoanalysis and anthropology. Among her findings is the insight that "what is important about a computer is the machine's ability to embody a process and to specify a sequence of rules. . . . And thinking about the core of a machine as the exercise of logic leads people back to thinking of the computer as mind." Still, if pressed, everyone knows and admits that a computer is not really a mind, or even a true intelligence. As one observer reported to Turkle, "Computers are programmed; people aren't. . . . [Computers] do only what they are programmed to do, nothing more and nothing less." People and real minds do not. Computers have no soul, no spirit.[10]

Nevertheless, those who have reflected on the operations of very complex computer systems speak of very extraordinary kinds of programming that produce unusual logics — the logics of what some commentators have called a "society." It is a "society" in the sense that it is a dynamic, ordered, yet unpredictable interaction of "multiple, simultaneously interacting programs."[11] This sort of "society" seems to have a kind of consciousness, one that early in the history of computers led Norbert Wiener to theological reflections in his book *God and Golem, Inc.*,[12] and one that younger "hackers" think about as a kind of "soul" in the machine. As Turkle points out, "They lose themselves in the idea of mind building mind and in the sense of merging their minds with a universal system. . . . Because they stand on the line between mind and not-mind, between life and not-life [in a way quite different from the Bomb] computers excite reflection about the nature of mind and the nature of life."[13]

Some begin to think of the self as a very complex and constantly changing intersection of logics, ever creating new mind-building possibilities, while others tend to understand society itself as a complex system of multiple logics where parts can reprogram and get feedback from other parts and constantly correct one another in the construction of new models of interacting. Societal creation and the constant recreation of the parts within a system then become a new technique — part skill, part art, part science,

---

10. Turkle, *The Second Self: Computers and the Human Spirit* (New York: Simon & Schuster, 1984), p. 274.

11. Turkle, *The Second Self,* p. 276.

12. Wiener, *God and Golem, Inc.: A Comment on Certain Points Where Cybernetics Impinges on Religion* (Cambridge: MIT Press, 1964).

13. Turkle, *The Second Self,* p. 32 and elsewhere.

and part transformed consciousness — that we do not understand scientifically and cannot fully control technologically.

If this is so, it does not seem unreasonable to take some of Norbert Wiener's reflections with great seriousness. As the founder of cybernetics, he showed that it was possible for lower energy systems with higher levels (indeed, abstract levels) of principle and purpose to control lower-level systems of higher energy and lack of direction, yet the logic of the lower-level systems shapes and limits the capacity of higher-level systems to function. A simple example is that of a driver on the road. A small section of the driver's brain controls the musculature of the eye, which, when it perceives something on the road, transmits messages to the larger leg muscles that control the accelerator and the brake, which in turn control the several-thousand-pound machine hurtling down the turnpike. The key in this example is how accurate the eye's perception of reality is, and how well the information perceived is interpreted and coordinated with the other larger muscle groups to control the mechanics of the automobile. The "logic" of each part influences the behavior of the whole.

More significant, as Wiener suggests, is that the highest-level logics, which are in many ways the least potent, are the most important to the whole. When this understanding is transferred to an understanding of "societal mind," we find ourselves confronted with the question of what basic logics of meaning, what governing principles and purposes are in interaction with and coordinate the much larger energy systems that have no control mechanisms of their own. We are on the brink of theological questions. At the highest level, the logic of our metaphysical-moral vision is decisive, and the way that level relates to material systems is both something of a mystery and something decisive for the trajectory of technological civilization.

The import of these reflections for us is that the churches, dealing with what can only be described as relatively low-energy systems of rather high-level "abstract" symbols, perceptions, and dynamic logics of interpretation and guidance, often program the destiny of entire systems — often almost unwittingly and before reflection. Earlier I suggested that our response to the question of the bomb might have something to do with *sacrament*. Since making that suggestion, I have argued that the other major symbol of modern technology, the computer, requires taking a theological approach to the highest levels of abstraction, those that can be related to a "societal mind."

Now I want to connect these two ideas by calling again on the notion of a public theology, that portion of it which points to the importance of liturgies, rites, and rituals.

SACRAMENTAL SYMBOLS
IN A TECHNOLOGICAL SOCIETY

In religion, sacrament is the primal form of technique—it is the skill and the art by which we symbolize the most profound connections between the most abstract logics of meaning and the realities of the material world. Further, sacraments and the more important rites are performed when we do not know the future and cannot tell whether it will lead to life and new societies of meaning or death and the destruction of meaning. Christians baptize in hope, but without assurance, to signify a physical change of status (birth or adulthood), an alteration of social membership (induction into the community of faith), and a transformed orientation to an insecure future—an orientation marked, we pray, by a new discipline, a wider concern for others, and a deeper loyalty to God.

The other great sacrament, communion, particularly looks forward to the inclusive eschatological banquet, even when there is little assurance of a real future in this world. It takes the products of nature, changed by art and technique into bread and wine, and transforms them into symbols of eschatological meaning and social solidarity, even where the empirical evidence that history will bring a time of full sharing with plenty for all is uncertain. In such sacramental actions we nevertheless claim that a metaphysical-moral meaning ultimately governs and guides life and the patterns of our interactions, and that we know enough about its character to proleptically enact that ultimate meaning symbolically in the present. We affirm that whatever the future brings, we will face it in solidarity with the community of the saints over the centuries and in all countries, and that we will strive to form a common "societal mind" with them, whatever our various logics. Although we ourselves are less than saintly, in these actions we pledge ourselves to enter into a community of the committed that will witness to the whole earth. And we participate in such symbolic actions because we believe that it is possible for humans to know, in materially based experience, something of the ultimate basis for ultimate meaning, and we know that this allows and demands the material alteration of our conditions—of our bodies, our time, our finances, our energy, our will, and our world. We must share in that which feeds body, community, and spirit.

To my knowledge, none of the great founders of modern theology have addressed public issues of political economy in a sacramental way. Fundamentalists are suspicious of sacrament, most evangelicals neglect it, and much of ecumenical Protestant thought relegates it to "practical theology" in a condescending way. A good bit of Catholic sacramental theology seems focused on the legalistic structures of priestly practice, and Orthodox sacramental thought remains wrapped in such antiquarian modes of expression that those most deeply involved in it have seldom tried to spell out its implications for the peculiar problems of modernity. Even less attention has been given to the potential implications of the rites and rituals of non-Christian religions for technological life, perhaps because many are so much related to ontocratic assumptions that the connections to technology are few.

Of course, the rites and rituals of various civil religions do have very strong technological elements, but these are most frequently related to the celebration of armaments. Civil holidays are marked by military parades, national leaders are honored with twenty-one-gun salutes, and many of every nation's most sacred monuments are to those who led and those who died in war. Every social unit, including the nation-state, needs celebrative moments and festivals to cultivate solidarity and group consciousness, but the "sacraments" of civil religion are more likely to cultivate a spirituality approving of the bomb than of a global and ethical societal consciousness that prompts us to love our enemies.

Christian sacramental thinking may well have the potential — precisely because of its metaphysical, moral, societal, and cosmic content — to provide what is needed. The resources for a public theology are potentially enormous. However, until the multiple levels of meaning implicit in such thinking are sorted and refined by encounter with the basic questions of the relationship of technique to science, art, and social form, those closest to modern developments in technology can hardly fathom what all that "mystical stuff" is about.

One wishes that the deep implications of what is implicit in the best of Christian sacramental thought were spelled out with concrete reference to political-economic matters and especially technological matters. Perhaps it must become one of the primary tasks of our day to recover and recast a sacramental understanding of nature, society, "common mind," and the human future. Sacramental thought always has a high appreciation of creation, but it also knows that nature (and human nature) in its raw form is not sufficient. The careful and responsible transformation — even the transubstantiation — of biophysical reality is required. The new joint ecumenical studies on baptism and the Eucharist are promising,[14] but the larger implications have not yet been made explicit.

In holy communion the fruits of the earth, transformed by human hands and treated with holy regard in the midst of a transubstantial meeting of minds, are shared with all who earnestly repent of their sins and know they have need of spiritual and material sustenance. This sharing anticipates the banquet of gracious mutuality that God intends as human destiny. It is a theological paradigm for the way in which the corporate integration of technique, science, and art ought to intervene in nature, to reorder it according to a higher purpose and logic, and in the process knit together diverse patterns of thought into a dynamic society of coherent meaning and purpose that comprehends and integrates multiple diverse logics. Were the rich significance of sacramental actions spelled out and made living realities in modern technological societies, our stewardship of the Word might not only become enfleshed in ritual behaviors and liturgical forms. It might become publicly embodied in a more just, participatory, and sustainable technological civilization able to resist the temptation to use the bomb and less inclined to idolize artificial intelligence than to seek, trust, and honor the one Intelligence that stands behind it all.

Study Questions

As this chapter points out, technology is a key factor contributing to social change. It brings new promise and new perils. It reshapes our political and economic institutions; it redefines our relationship to nature.

1. How is technology different from "craft"? From science? From art?

2. Respond to this statement: "Science is the attempt to discover 'natural law.'" If nature works by an inevitable pattern of causation, what are we to think about human freedom? How can we develop a technology to change natural patterns?

---

14. See the World Council of Churches, *Baptism, Eucharist and Ministry* (Geneva: WCC Press, 1982).

3. Once technology gets started, does it tend to take over everything? Do you find modern technology to be frightening or hopeful? How do you assess its role in medicine? In space exploration? Do you think it dehumanizes life? Does it make life more humane?

4. Does technological change alter our ethics and our theology? Do developments in theology and ethics alter technology?

5. How does the creation of technology reflect the principle of vocation?

6. Many of the most advanced civilizations of the ancient world (those of Egypt, India, etc.) were not "Third World" in the modern sense. How have religious beliefs affected the patterns of social, political, technological, and economic change over time?

7. Do you think "nature" is "fallen"? Do you think that people can and should reorder things in a way that is in some sense "less fallen"?

8. What are the criteria by which we can judge the merit of one technology over another?

9. Does the threat of human annihilation by means of nuclear weapons also imperil faith? How is theology to respond to such perils?

10. Do computers and other similar communications technologies have any social, ethical, and spiritual implications?

11. Do you agree that the sacraments have implications for the stewardship of our modern, technologized political economy? What have you been taught about the meanings of the sacraments? What do you want your children to learn about them?

12. What is the meaning of baptism in your tradition? Are there other meanings that can and should be spelled out for a public theology today? What can your tradition contribute to the ecumenical understanding of baptism in a time when young people must confront the realities of a high-tech civilization?

13. What is the meaning of communion in your tradition? Are there other meanings that can and should be identified today? What can your tradition learn about communion from other traditions and from a theologically concerned social analysis?

14. In the final analysis, is it not true that symbolic actions and religious rituals are really powerless in the face of modern technology? If so, why perform them? If not, what difference can they make?

CHAPTER NINE

Pluralism and the Future of Stewardship

What we have discussed so far in this book reflects the fact that both modern theology as it bears on public life and political economies as they are shaped by modern complex societies are inevitably pluralistic and dynamic. Diversity, not conformity, is the dominant mark of modern life; dynamic change, not fixed stability, is the character of social existence. Perhaps no societies in the history of humanity have been as pluralistic and dynamic as modern ones. Indeed, the terms "pluralistic" and "dynamic" have become not only descriptive of the ways things are but prescriptive of the way things ought to be. If we are to be stewards in and stewards of modern society, we will need to be guided by a pluralistic and dynamic theological framework related to a dynamic, pluralistic social analysis.

None except the most vicious tyrants want an authoritarian society, a totalitarian state, a monopolistic economy, or a technology operating in one fixed mode. Indeed, everywhere these occur, the despots who dominate such civilizations always argue that what they do is necessary only because the culture, the political order, the economic situation, or some other social sphere is temporarily in such dire straits that only by a necessary but abnormal tyranny can everything be saved from disintegration. It is always an "emergency," not "normal" life, that is used as a rationale for the denial of pluralism. Enforced conformity is set forth as a means for reestablishing enough integrity that diversity may flourish, eventually, on a new foundation. All over the world—from Afghanistan to Nicaragua, from Libya to South Africa, from Iran to Korea, from Chile to Indonesia — centralized authoritarian governments recapitulate the theme: the radical accent on unity is but one aspect of the quest for a "genuine" pluralism — one that will not fall apart by intolerable fragmentation, and one that is not merely polarized into contending forces.

PLURALISM: A BLESSING AND A CURSE

As we saw earlier, the metaphysical-moral notion of pluralism with unity and coherence with diversity has given rise, politically, to "constitutional democracy." Everyone at least claims to be working toward the goal of true democracy — one that involves a pluralism within a moral, social, and legal coherence and that provides protection for minorities, dissent, and opposition. Economically, the quest for pluralism and unity has given rise to "corporate capitalism" within a society, which also regulates economic activity and provides protection and opportunity for those disadvantaged by the actions of the market. But this structure, as we have seen, is potentially troublesome, precisely because the "capitalist" side of it can degenerate into individualistic competition that loses coherence, and because the "corporate" side of it can easily become so attached to dominant elites of *oikos* or *polis* that no effective pluralism is preserved. And technologically, pluralism is endemic to those societies in which multiple means of communication form a new "societal mind," and it is threatened by the proliferation of those kinds of technological armament that make all forms of life potential victims.

Pluralism is also understood to be a blessing in civilizations such as the modern West and in religious groupings such as the ecumenical churches, where leadership has begun to attend to previously neglected voices. When we hear of the concerns of women, blacks, Hispanics, Asians, and Native Americans, some of which are expressions of pain or anger induced by the imperious dogmatisms of white, male elites, we can celebrate pluralism. The insights, experiences, and wisdom brought into common discourse; the talents, hopes, and energy brought into common activities; and the commitment, gifts, and enthusiasm brought into common institutions — these contributions by previously excluded peoples diversify and enrich ranges of life that may have spoken of pluralism but exemplified monolithic domination.

Social pluralism is also a blessing when it provides multiple opportunities for the development of the human personality. When it is possible, for example, to be gainfully employed, to construct something useful, to hear good music, to participate in political decisions that affect the larger community, to experience the love and tenderness of family and friends, to read a good book, to see a good show, and to enjoy physical exercise in the course of day-to-day living, the human personality is enhanced. The mind, the body, and the spirit are enriched. Such diversities of daily life evoke a greater wholeness in life. All religions, cultures, and civilizations find it constrictive if people are denied such a pluralism of opportunity, or if people become so intensely committed to one thing that they become unresponsive to any others. Kierkegaard's notion that purity of heart is to will one thing is valid only if that one thing is sufficiently multifaceted to allow pluralistic fulfillment.

As it turns out, pluralism and its dynamism can also be a curse. When pluralism becomes an idol invoked to defend a universal normlessness, it becomes positively perverse. If we worship at the altar of anomie, claiming that everything anybody believes is so subjective that we can say nothing about anything with security, there is no reason even to take this god seriously. If everything is so completely "perspectival" that we cannot imagine anything to be true or just or right or good in itself, we face the same problem that Heraclitus faced long ago when he argued that everything is in such a state of flux that we can never step into the same river twice. Yet he wanted to claim that the "fluxus quo" was eternally true and more valid than any other perspective. He did not quite recognize what Einstein seems to have recognized in the twentieth century: that even dealing with relativity demands acknowledgment that reality in flux has constant and pervasive patterns of coherence rooted in a stable, transcendent reality. "I shall never believe," he said, "that God plays dice with the world."

The view that nothing could be true or just or right or good in any constant or knowable way, that everything depends on the immediate demands of the situation and on the perspective from which we see it, does indeed lead to a kind of dynamic pluralism. But it is a pluralism that surely cannot guide our thought or our lives in the cosmopolitan world of modern political economy. It implies that no vision of God, humanity, or the world could be judged to be any more valid than any other view, and that what we have is some passing opinion or contextual eruption that has no claim on us and for which no warrants could be given. Some of us are Methodists and some of us are Baptists, some Buddhists and some Marxists, some liberals and some conservatives, some fascists and some feminists — and there we are. No group is more right or more wrong than any other. In philosophy, Nietzsche stands as the great advocate of this view, called nihilism. It posits that those with the greatest "will" come to dominate everything.

Such a view of pluralism is a threat to the stewardship of modern societies. Every civilization seems to need, at its core, a metaphysical-moral vision, a spiritual and ethical guidance system that provides some clues about how to structure the diversities and dynamisms of the common life so that they do not pull it apart at the seams. If such guidance is not provided, coercive power, economic influence, and technology driven by imperialistic will will decide everything for arbitrary, self-serving reasons.

Two contemporary studies help us see some of the dynamics involved here. One is *Habits of the Heart* by Robert Bellah and others.[1] Bellah and his colleagues offer an interpretation of the contemporary ethos of middle-class society that I find difficult to refute. Bellah argues that we as a people have lost what rootage we had earlier from biblical insights and from classical attempts to define "public virtues." Combined, these once provided us with a public theology. But today things are much different. The research reported in this book renders a picture of individualistic relativism taking the forms of "therapeutic expressivism" and "managerial utilitarianism," which are rampant in our culture. The first is basically psychological and deals with the expression of inner values we hold because of their importance to our preferred life-styles. The second reflects the commercial, contractual way we make deals with one another and manipulate our environments to get material results supportive of our interests. These "therapeutic" and "managerial" models of meaning render us incapable of imagining that anything is true or right or just or good in any objective sense. Such views provide no possible range of discourse by which we could discuss the question of whether humans are accountable before any higher laws or ultimate purposes amid the complex institutions of modern society. Large segments of the population seem to have lost what Bellah calls the "second language" of metaphysics, morality, and theology, and have only a primal language of feeling and problem-solving. Many caught in the modern web of therapeutic-managerial models of reality may feel themselves to be

---

1. Bellah et al., *Habits of the Heart: Individualism and Commitment in American Life* (Berkeley and Los Angeles: University of California Press, 1984).

religious, but in such a context religion itself becomes primarily a means of adjusting the self to the world or the world to the self. If Bellah is correct, it makes little sense to claim that humans are to be stewards of any "Word" that ought to become incarnate in political, economic, or modern technological life because it is true and just and right and good.

Such observations as these drive us back to themes discussed in the first chapter. If it is not possible to articulate, defend, and embody a public theology in personal and social existence, the churches ought to close their doors, or admit that they have nothing substantive to offer the world beyond what modernity already offers the affluent, and simply become centers for cheap therapy and self-help techniques, probably on a fee-for-service basis. But if the churches know, by a critically examined faith, something that is true and right and good and just, then they become absolutely indispensable to modernity. Our stewardship of a public theology demands that we become shapers of, advocates for, and active organizers of communities dedicated to a public theology.

On a quite different level — the international, cross-cultural one — similar problems confront us. These are powerfully articulated by Wilfred Cantwell Smith in *The Meaning and End of Religion.*[2] Having spent years engaging in the comparative analysis of the world's religions, Smith writes on the phenomenon of faith in a way that reflects and clarifies a great number of current attitudes among those who do want to take religion seriously and who attempt to find a holistic, nonjudgmental way of seeing the variety of faiths. Smith thinks that faith is to be seen as a personal act of existential trust in an "Absolute." What is decisive about faith has nothing to do with the doctrines, the sacramental practices, or the cognitive claims of the various world religions. These are entirely variable and contextually determined, and no one religion can ever be seen to be more true or just or right or good than any other one. The several traditions of the world's religions are simply aspects of the one history of human faith. "Faithing" is what is important; the content of faith is irrelevant.

But it is doubtful whether this view is quite so open to pluralism as it seems. It may simply homogenize the psychodynamics of faith. It does not appear to take seriously the fact that each of the world's religions makes truth claims and does not view itself

2. Smith, *The Meaning and End of Religion* (New York: New American Library, 1963).

as but one incidental case of a general experience of faithing in
which all cases are equal. Nor does this view take seriously the fact
that the content of particular faiths is decisive for the shape of
civilizations, and that some faiths allow pluralism within coherent
unities, and others disallow it. Indeed, what is likely is that Smith
has imposed a worldview on the various religions that suggests
that most of what their adherents think, do, believe, and practice
is irrelevant. Certainly such a view does not help us understand
the ways in which some religions incline to a coherent pluralism in
society and history while others seem to press toward despotism
or chaos.

If, however, we begin to look at the structures of social history
as influenced by religion from the standpoint of a public theology,
we will have to ask more fundamental questions about the nature
and character of pluralism than are present either in the social
psychology of modern therapeutic and managerial views of pluralism (in which pluralism has become such an idol that we doubt the
reality of anything that speaks of truth and justice), or in the attitudes we often have about the relativity of the world's religions.
What we often see in these forms of pluralism leads directly to
relativism, to normlessness.

It may be that parts of the Christian tradition, and especially
aspects of Protestantism, are responsible for the contemporary tendency toward relativism. More than half a century ago, Paul Tillich
announced "the end of the Protestant era."[3] He noted that the prophetic impulse of Christianity, which took on a vibrant new form
in the Reformation, issued in the "Protestant Principle." This principle has served as a legacy to all religions and civilizations. Nothing in nature, nothing in history, and nothing devised by human
invention can capture and exhaust the transcendent reality of God.
A prophetic distrust of every human formulation, theory, and social
order is thus intrinsic to every profound and valid movement.

And yet we have reached "the end" of the Protestant era. This
is so because large portions of Protestantism have proven to be
incapable of setting forth a constructive view of how the message
they confess can be validated, and how it might inform cultures,
philosophies, the sciences, and the fabric of social life. Protestantism can, on the basis of its grasp of the principle of protest, offer
a critique of the idolatries and ideologies of civilization. But exclu-
sive accent on the protesting spirit makes it nearly impossible to

---

3. Tillich, *The Protestant Era* (Chicago: University of Chicago Press, 1948).

speak constructively to those responsible for political, economic, technological, scientific, and artistic structures. However critical we may wish to be of Tillich on other grounds, it may well be that he has identified a problem of considerable importance. We may have to seek various "forms of grace" in thought and society that allow us to preserve the pluralism and dynamism of modern life, but that also give them a coherence beyond diversity, which can so easily degenerate into anomie.

If we are to articulate and defend a Trinitarian theology today and to claim that it is pertinent to public discourse, to modern political economics, we will have to take another step. We will have to show that a fundamental pluralism within a coherent unity is necessary to the public institutions of life.

THE NECESSARY PLURALISM OF SOCIETY

Surely it is possible to argue that inherent in every human civilization is a tendency to plurality, one that requires a certain pluralism of institutional formation. This is true because we humans are multifaceted creatures with multiple roles that we must carry out if we are to be whole persons and if we are to live in viable communities. A failure to preserve a diversity of structures and dynamics leads to tyranny. A failure to see how these diversities can and should be ordered coherently leads to anarchy. This is true theologically and personally. It is certainly the case socially. Every human civilization has to have certain core institutions. No society can survive over time if any of these fail.

The first indispensable institution is family. We humans are sexual creatures, and everywhere males and females find ways to get together. Yet the dynamics of our sexuality are multifaceted. If there are no ways of ordering these relationships, exploitation and domination on one side or confusion and disorder on the other disrupt our emotions, our daily patterns of life, and the destinies of our children.

A second necessary structure for community is a political edifice. No society is sufficiently without the threat of violence from within or without that it can survive without some ways of structuring authority to defend the community — with force if necessary — and to demand contributions to the commonweal necessary for social survival and well-being.

Still a third functional requirement of every civilization is an economy. This means that we must have both specific institutions set aside to produce goods and services for all other sectors of society, and a technological way of getting and distributing resources from the biophysical world that forms community (i.e., forms a "societal mind" that takes account of multiple logics and does not destroy the ecosphere).

And in all the above areas, some conventional means of communication is required to allow the expression of meanings experienced therein. In short, a family system, a system of governance, a system of production and distribution, and a cultural-linguistic system are indispensable to human existence. Where one or more of these break down from the inside or are destroyed from the outside, civilization collapses.

However, each of these institutions has different dynamics that pull in different directions. No effort to separate males and females by building economic, political, and cultural systems to prevent their contact has ever worked for long. No plan to prevent cultural borrowing or to keep economic resources entirely within some political or clan-familial system has ever been effective over time. New families, different political factions, divergent economic interests and classes, and dissenting subcultures always develop. Attempts to hold one of these systems in check by the constraints of another never become fully operative, although such efforts make life incredibly difficult for a time. Indeed, something is lost to civilization if any one of these systems is collapsed into one or several of the others. If, for example, family life becomes only a means of economic gain, political power, or adaptation to cultural stereotypes, something of the innate dynamic of human sexuality is destroyed and is likely to appear in distorted forms elsewhere in the society. If political life becomes wholly subservient to another system — the familial and sexual, the economic, or the cultural — the capacity to make balanced political decisions is undercut. And we have already argued that if economic or technological areas of life become totally dominated by familial, political, or cultural institutions, they begin to destroy more than they construct.

In most civilizations, what holds these divergent systems together is religion — the fifth necessary institution of human existence in community. To be sure, religion has often been identified with the patriarchy (or, occasionally, the matriarchy) of the family or with the ecstasy of reproduction itself, with the dominion of the regime or with the lust for power itself, with success of some economic class or with the process of production itself, and with the language of some particular people or with the muses who inspire poetry, song, and dance. But religion at its deeper levels claims to point to another dimension of meaning that gives order to — and not only reflects the order of — these areas of existence. Indeed, every religion that finds it possible to shape civilizational life finds that it must have a way of coherently guiding yet keeping distinct the necessarily plural institutions of life.

In its long history, Christianity has resisted the identification of its faith and its characteristic institution, the church, with any one of these other institutions. Some of the most decisive debates in our past are precisely debates about how much we should sanctify some particular familial, political, economic, or cultural system. We have faltered often, but the most remarkable thing about Christianity looked at from this angle is that it has never been entirely swallowed up by one or another of these systems. Most of the reform movements in the history of the faith, in fact, have come from some effort to reassert the core vision of the truth and justice of God that some part of the church thinks is in danger of being subverted by becoming merely an ideological appendage to one or another of these systems. The church is not patriarchy, the tribe, or the clan, although it can be a model for and give guidance to the family. The church is not governance, rule, political power, or party, although it may speak with authority, develop a polity, and shape the common patterns of law and order. The church is not a class, a system of production, or economic prudence, although it can exercise influence by the way it preaches, teaches, and acts with regard to the accumulation and disposition of wealth, and by offering a covenantal model for corporate life. Nor does the church provide a technique or a technology, although it may engender a sacramental attitude toward the cosmos and the ethos that makes a just, sustainable, and participatory technology possible. And the church is not a culture, a linguistic system, or poetry, although it can utilize a thousand of these forms to express what it is about.

Nevertheless, while the church is not any of these systems, the main traditions of Christianity have agreed that certain societal structures have to be recognized by everyone, whether they are religious or not, Christian or not. Christians have spoken of these in a variety of ways. The Catholic tradition saw in the "natural law" certain marks of God's creative intent that could also be recognized by human reason and conscience. The Reformers often spoke of "the ordinances of God," communal patterns of life based on the law of the Creator God that were binding on all human creatures. Others spoke of the "orders" or "estates" of creation, or of the "spheres of relative sovereignty," or of the "mandates" that God has established to preserve life. These doctrinal formulations have been abused often, and there is incomplete agreement about how they can best be understood. But they all point to an important fact of created human existence: there are multiple dimensions of life that we cannot alter yet in which we have some relative degree of freedom. And we can use that freedom to destroy the integrity of these patterns and subvert the very fabric of human life.

To maintain pluralism and to give it coherent order, the church must take its primary clues from those parts of doctrine which are not simply the reflection of the current structures of core institutions, and which can give normative shape to these several sectors in a way that allows the diversities of human existence to find expression in the current contexts of life.

Here, then, we begin to see one area of stewardship that has been on the agenda of the past and that is now on the agenda of the future: the continued cultivation and refinement of a public theology that can give coherence to the pluralism of the core institutions of life in a way that can sustain the necessarily pluralistic structure of people's lives in a great variety of societies, cultures, and subcultures. Today we might all recognize the pluralism of these core institutions in indirect ways. Newspapers and magazines often have specific sections dealing with each of these. There are distinctive architectural patterns for homes, government buildings, factories and stores, theaters, and religious institutions. And we note that we conduct ourselves according to values that vary somewhat, depending on whether we are in a family situation, in a political campaign, at work, at a concert, or at church. And yet we are unsure about what can give integrative coherence to these pluralistic institutions so that humanity can avoid the perennial terrors of tyranny and chaos. It is unlikely that the therapeutic or the managerial models that are currently widespread can sustain society over time without inducing fragmentation, and it is improbable that a confidence in "faithing" will help us find coherence if that faithing has no substantive content. Nor will reliance on only the Protestant principle help us as it may have helped those in the past. A constructive vision of possible forms of grace is required.

Indeed, the need is urgent, because today we are confronted with another dimension of pluralism that compounds our difficulties and that has great implications for both stewardship and the political economy. Not only must we continually replenish and develop a public theology that can critically evaluate patterns in familial, political, economic, technological, and cultural life, but we must face new complexities of pluralism that are as yet less well-defined.

I refer to the professions. The life roles, the institutional formations, and the alterations of both personal identity and social structure implied by reference to the development of the modern professions are as dramatic as any other developments in society except, perhaps, technology and the corporation, to which the professions are intimately related.

THE PROFESSIONS:
THE NEW COMPLEXITIES OF PLURALISM

We can get some sense of what is implied by the rise of the professions if we trace, briefly, how they developed and how they have influenced the core institutions of society. As already noted, every civilization must have a way of dealing with family life, political authority, economic productivity, and cultural activity. Each must also have a metaphysical-moral vision to hold these diverse aspects of human life in some compelling, coherent pattern of meaning, while giving them arenas of the social cosmos in which the proper ends and dynamics of each may be pursued without undue constriction by the others. In the history of the West, the church has been the primary carrier of this vision. But the church has also been one of the key institutions in promoting still another layer of social and institutional development that produced the modern professions and modified the whole pattern.

Wherever the church has gone, it has promoted the development of schools, and with them the profession of teaching. From the earliest documents of the church, which were used for *didache,* it is clear that some leaders felt that they had a vocation, a calling from God, to engage in the teaching of the youth and the preparation of leadership for the future. Of course, every complex civilization has specialized institutions for the nurture of the young and the training of scholars, but these are almost always centered in *oikos* or *polis:* witness the father in ancient India hiring a guru to enter his home and teach his children, the clan in ancient China sending its bright young men to study at a court school, and the members of tribal religions sending off their youth for initiation. These forms of instruction functioned essentially to integrate the student into the classical wisdom and traditional lore of the caste, the state, or the tribe. Although parallels can be found in the West, more remarkable is the establishment of schools distinct from these practices. It is in these schools that the intellectual life of modernity developed.

What was important about these schools is that they were distinct in principle and in social organization from the core institutions of life and thus provided an arena of critical learning that took the student outside of the direct control of those institutions. Schools abstract people from their primary involvements and allow them to develop analytical tools with which to critically evaluate the structures and dynamics of the core institutions.

Wherever the church has gone during the centuries of its expansion, it has always developed schools, and it has done so in considerable tension with the prevailing familial, political, economic, and cultural patterns of the day. Even today, new church-sponsored missionary movements — whether home or foreign — almost immediately establish schools staffed by professional educators. This heritage is so deep that even where public schools and universities are established by governments, and where parents are sometimes deeply involved in deciding aspects of the curriculum, the professionals are granted a degree of independent control over standards, curriculum, evaluation, and quality.

Law is a second professional area that has been deeply influenced by theology and the church, and its modern elaborations have been decisive for many of the structures of modern societies.[4] In most civilizations, law is what the political rulers say it is, often (to be sure) as advised by those representing the wisdom of the culture — sages, elders, and poets — and more often as influenced by those who control large chunks of the economy; but in the religions that derive from the biblical traditions, the basic principles of law are thought to have a divine origin to which political leaders, wise-men, and the worldly wise also are supposed to be obedient. Since the formations of canon law and the training of professionals who specialized in its interpretation and application, often in direct conflict both with the "civil laws" propagated by political authority and with the nearly sovereign authority of the father's word in all domestic matters, law and the professionals who practice it have been seen as dependent on transcendent standards of right and wrong, fairness and justice. The notions of professional standards and the "independence" of the judiciary are but two modern man-

---

4. See H. J. Berman, *Law and Revolution: The Formation of the Western Legal Tradition* (Cambridge: Harvard University Press, 1983).

ifestations of this long historical development. This understanding of law implies a certain abstraction from the core communities in which we live most of our lives.

A third professional area influenced by the church is medicine. There are witch doctors and healers in every culture, but historically hospitals have been established by the churches. From the founding of the orders of "hospitalers" before the Crusades to the founding of hospitals in "newer lands" by denominations as a part of their ministry, the church has been a primary force in the formation of the modern professions of medicine. Indeed, medicine — like education, law, and ministry — has been treated as one of the classical "vocations" that gave rise to the modern professions. And everywhere that Christianity has gone in its worldwide ministries, it has trained nurses, doctors, and paramedics, established clinics and homes for the elderly and the severely ill, and founded hospitals of all kinds.

Yet a fourth professional area has developed, the one least directly influenced by the church: engineering. Indirectly, of course, the witness of the church has been of great importance here too. The Christian belief that nature is both rational and "fallen" and thus can be altered to be brought into accord with God's plans for human salvation implicitly supports engineering. Further, the institutions of education, law, and medicine fostered by the church developed ways of thinking about problems which themselves gave impetus to the transformation of traditional scientific techniques — notwithstanding the celebrated cases, such as that of Galileo, in which the church resisted new scientific developments.

Whatever the historical case, it is surely true that today the various technical professions related to business, governmental services, industry, and technology are considered to be viable Christian vocations to which some are called, and that work in these areas also involves a certain abstraction from ordinary ways of thinking about life, nature, society, and human destiny. As we have seen, the institutional arena in which these professions are predominantly practiced today is the corporation. Indeed, most schools and universities, hospitals and medical research centers, and law firms are organized as corporations.

For our purposes, what is remarkable about the development of these professions is the fact that they alter the structure and dynamics of every one of the core institutions. Children are sent to school, given over to the hands of experts, outside the direct control of parents, cultural sage, or economic interest. Even the state must in some measure respect "academic freedom." Sick people are sent to a hospital, suspected criminals to a court, and both managers and workers go to the corporation to do their work. Each of these institutions is also distinct in principle from the influence of the other social institutions and from the direct control of any of the other professional institutions. Thus, in addition to those core patterns of organizational pluralism necessary to every society, an additional layer of structural pluralism is built into modern societies. "Professional" institutions become necessary for the survival of modern complex social systems. Complex civilizations depend to a great degree on the health and performance of these professional sectors of modern life. If any of these groups — educational systems and teachers, judicial systems and lawyers, hospitals and medical personnel, or corporations and engineers — fails, is corrupted, or attempts to take control of the whole of society, it threatens the civilization.

The story of the professionalization of life is as yet unfinished. It is occurring at astonishing rates around the world. The mark of being modern, both in changing traditional societies and in capitalist and socialist contexts, is the development of indigenous universities, hospitals, and organizations of professional lawyers and engineers. Leaders of developing countries who protest the alteration of their traditional cultures by alien influences nevertheless make every effort to adopt as quickly as possible the institutional patterns and professional expertise these influences entail. Liberals, conservatives, progressives, radicals, and reactionaries rail against the undue influence of university eggheads, fat-cat lawyers, money-hungry doctors, and uncouth technocrats. Nevertheless, they are delighted to share the news with all their friends when their daughter or son becomes a professional in one or another of these fields and joins this or that faculty, law office, medical staff, corporate bureaucracy, or engineering firm.

Furthermore, the refinements of professionalization increase at every turn. One does not simply become a teacher anymore; one becomes a teacher in political science, the arts, economics, science, or some other field. And seldom does one simply practice law in general. Rather, one becomes a constitutional lawyer, a corporation lawyer, a lawyer specializing in forensic medicine, or a patent lawyer. General practitioners in medicine are fewer and farther between, and the subdivisions in the engineering sciences are as numerous as the departments at MIT.

Nor should we fail to mention that professionalization has

spilled over into every other arena of life and grown throughout the various socioeconomic classes. Professional organizations have developed for hairdressers, music managers, basketball players, traffic controllers, junk dealers, and insurance salespersons, to mention only a few. And what self-respecting parents today would presume to raise their children without regularly consulting at least the manuals written by child psychologists, development experts, and a myriad of other specialists? Such pluralization of the professions not only influences the fabric of society but has direct implications for the way in which we conceive of and live our lives in modern political economies. All of these areas of professional activity are, in some direct senses, independent of both traditional *oikos* and political control, yet they have an enormous impact on family life, the cultural-linguistic systems by which we communicate, the formation of political attitudes, and the shape of technology. Neither the ideologies of classical socialism nor the ideologies of classical capitalism seem capable of dealing with the import of these developments.

We have begun to produce an "expert" society, with each person knowing and able to do something important for the whole, even if each has little conception of the whole and how his or her part contributes to it. That which, in the past, provided a vision of the whole — religion — is itself relegated to another kind of specialization, one that does not relate very directly to what most people do with most of their time and most of their psychic energy. The clergy are seldom equipped to speak to the kinds of issues that the various professionals confront in their daily lives. Indeed, most clergy cannot understand what most people do. All this is, of course, directly pertinent to the question of what is demanded of us in a public theology.

Between the Reformation and these modern developments, the Christian doctrines of vocation and covenant played particularly decisive roles in forming the institutions of modernity. The former accented the notion that God calls each person to specific duties and roles in the world and gives each the gifts necessary to carry them out. The "calling" to ministry was broadened to the "priesthood of all believers" and eventually to the vocation of every individual, a vocation to be properly responded to by a "profession" of faith lived out in diligent service under the laws and purposes of God. The doctrine of covenant accented the propriety of forming communities of discipline to engage in mutual edification and action, and also to serve the laws and purposes of God by serving humanity. Vocation and covenant as the personal and social dimensions of the obedient stewardship of life issued in the formation of professional institutions that transformed modernity in a pluralistic direction while providing a larger unifying vision of responsibility to the whole.[5]

In recent years, however, the idea of vocation has been replaced by the idea of career as the governing notion of professional life. And the idea of covenant has been replaced by the idea of contract. "Career" comes from a word that referred to the race course in the ancient Roman world. It is a word that refers to achievement by competitive combat, getting ahead, and triumphing over others — even if such achievement involves merely going around in circles. The echoes of this word can be found linguistically — we speak of "careening" around corners, for example — and substantively: we may refer to our profession as a "rat race." The word "contract" refers to the utilitarian agreements between parties whereby we establish a give-and-take relationship in which goods or services are exchanged on a tit-for-tat basis. A contract is made between individuals, and the rules of the contract are established by the parties themselves. By contrast, a covenant presumes that all such interactions have to be worked out under a higher law and for the larger good of the community.

This "secularization" of vocation and covenant into career and contract has made it possible for Hindus, Buddhists, Muslims, and humanists to participate in the patterns that were earlier established on Christian theological grounds, and some scholars think that the more these patterns of professionalism develop and are adopted by peoples of other religions, the more the residual ferment of Christian presuppositions will serve as a leaven in the loaf of other civilizations. Others argue that the theological foundations are best left behind altogether, and that the professions must proceed on a nontheological foundation, basing their developments on purely rational and empirical grounds, with each profession granted its own autonomy.

This proposal, however, is not feasible. Take a situation in a teaching hospital as an example. When doctors, social workers, family therapists, and nurses face the problem of whether or not to keep a seriously ill patient on a high-tech life-support system, educational, legal, medical, and technological questions may not

---

5. See John Weagraff, "Covenant and Vocation: Toward a Theologically Informed Social Ethic for the Professions," Ph.D. diss., Boston College, 1987.

converge. And to the degree that they might, they may be in conflict with cultural values, family desires, or economic feasibility. An integrated decision has to be made. And what is likely, should there be no integrating metaphysical-moral vision to guide these professionals, is that the professionals and their institutions will fall apart or be mandated in a particular direction by political authority. The goals of these various professions and professional institutions are often not the same. They pull in different directions, and sometimes they operate according to different understandings of life. And if there is no governing public theology, government is likely to enforce decisions in actions that would undercut the relative independence of the professions and thereby the pluralistic fabric of modern political economies.

Just as important for the churches, however, is what pluralism on all these levels means in regard to the stewardship of our lives. It means at least that our people are confronted with changing patterns in every sector of life and a vast array of possibilities. It also means that, for many, achievement in a career becomes the main purpose of life, and all relationships are contractual ones, subject to renegotiation if the price is right. Indeed, believers are tempted to use the church as a possible resource for enhancing a career or for making the right contacts.

In recent years, the churches have rather creatively focused on those who have been left behind in the transition to modern complex civilizations: the lonely, the unemployed, the nonprofessionals, those who are powerless in political life, those caught in sexually stereotyped roles in family life, and those racially stereotyped by cultural definitions of what is good and evil. Even more, the churches have reached out to those simpler cultures disrupted and exploited by the more complex ones, and have attempted both to heed their cries and to remedy their distress — sometimes by sending experts in education, law, medicine, and engineering to aid the development of these cultures, and sometimes by becoming their advocates in national or international forums of all kinds. Indeed, where the core institutions of life have been so disrupted that life has tended to cave in on many, the churches have formed "base communities." In these, peoples caught in the throes of transition and oppression can re-establish some sense of core communal life and gain fresh control over the core institutions under severely adverse conditions.

But the churches have done much less in addressing the stewardship of the modern professions and the patterns of modern corporate and technological life to which they are related, and that now shape worldwide and continuously expanding political economies.

THE FUTURE OF STEWARDSHIP

I have tried to argue throughout this book that we are called to be, above all, stewards of the Word. And that entails the necessary reclaiming and recasting of a public theology out of the classical warrants of Scripture, Tradition, Reason, and Experience. This involves not only clarifying the great themes of perennial importance but relating them to a viable "Christian sociology" by extending and refining the efforts of those who struggled with these questions during the formation of the modern political economies in which we live.

But we cannot simply echo what they have said. The developments in recent decades — especially the awareness of cross-cultural interaction, the new doubts about the relationships of piety and politics, the enormously increased role of the corporation, the development of the bomb and the computer, and the professionalization of life — have altered many aspects of public life. If what we have said thus gives us an estimate of our past resources and present conundrums, it may be that we can responsibly link our theology to the structures and dynamics of the emerging political economy in a way that guides, refines, and selectively transforms that which is destructive and selectively sustains that which is creative and redemptive.

One of the first requirements would be the transformation of theological education in the seminaries and in the churches. The predominant current patterns of theological education do not prepare us for present challenges. Neither at the level of theology nor at the level of social analysis can we say that Christian leadership is, on the whole, prepared to understand the basic frameworks of thought that modern Christian stewardship requires. Seldom do pastors preach and teach about the fundamental dynamics and structures of modern society or the associated theological and ethical doctrines that have been developed over centuries. An enormous amount of what passes for theological education centers on the psychodynamics of pastoral care or on those skills useful for the maintenance of ecclesiastical institutions. Neither emphasis is entirely false, but much of both simply reflects the therapeutic-managerial presuppositions of our culture.[6]

Many of the current understandings of theology show a serious distrust of anything "abstract." And this may be the greatest crisis of all. We cannot wrestle with problems of modern education, international law, contemporary medicine, or complex technology from a theological or ethical point of view without a willingness to work at a relatively abstract level. Nor can we grasp the nature of the modern corporation, the threat of nuclear weaponry, the significance of the computer, the fabric of democracy, or the social import of the professions without developing general models of what these are and by what governing standards we might evaluate them and transform them. And even if we were to attain a certain level of general understanding about these issues by empirical studies, there is little evidence that we could address and assess them at the theological and ethical levels without an even more abstract method of wrestling with the basic questions of how humans might reliably know something of a publicly defensible nature about how to speak normatively to such matters in a pluralistic world. Above all, a metaphysical-moral vision, defensible before the courts of an apologetic and critical theology and ethics, is demanded if we hope to give any stewardly guidance to the whole.

For those of us who believe that the Trinitarian God is the true God, pluralism is a normative theological belief as well as an ethical or social belief. The metaphysical-moral grounds for dealing with pluralism are at hand. Pluralism within a dynamic unity, understood in terms of persons in community and the community of persons, may be the most important postbiblical contribution of Christian theology to the understanding of both Word and world. It bears on the public life of civilizations precisely because it gives metaphysical-moral articulation to the proper foundations and limits of pluralism. Christians oppose monolithic definitions of ultimate reality, but their pluralistic beliefs are governed by a broader belief in unity. The triune God is integrated. Thus polytheism, the theological form of pluralism without unity, is condemned as strongly as is imperious singleness without differentiation. In using these terms, we see that both pluralism and unity can become blessings or curses, depending on whether our view of pluralism has an

---

6. I have attempted to make some suggestions about these matters in the forthcoming study written with international consultants, *Apologia: Contextualization, Globalization, and Mission in Theological Education.*

ultimate coherence and whether our view of unity has a place for diversity. It is not accidental that leading ecumenical bodies, as represented by the Faith and Order Commission of the World Council of Churches, have again taken up the question of how we are to deal with the great classical creeds — all of which are fundamentally Trinitarian.

If we are to articulate and defend a Trinitarian theology today and to claim that it is pertinent to public discourse, to modern political economics, we will have to take another step. We will have to show that a fundamental pluralism within a coherent unity is necessary to the public institutions of life. We will have to do what our forebears did when they developed the doctrine of the Trinity. In an entirely new cultural, social, and political environment, one whose terms of public discourse were not that of biblical confessionalism, they developed biblically based themes in new directions and linked them to nuanced analysis of the intellectual and social realities of current political and economic structures.

In the face of new contemporary structures of piety and power, spirituality and corporate life, and the development of computers and bombs, the chief task of Christian stewardship is the cultivation of a new public theology, rooted in disciplined but diverse communities of faith and service, and alert to the need for a new birth of cross-cultural and historically informed "Christian sociology." If this becomes intrinsic to the life of faith in our time, people will find a new sense of vocation that can give guidance to their lives, and new covenantal ways of struggling in community with the complexities of modern life. If the clergy link a Trinitarian theology to a new understanding of how modern societies work, we may find effective ways to assess and transform the dynamic and pluralistic structures of contemporary political economies. Then the people of God will be able to become stewards in deed.

Study Questions

One would think that modern politics, economics, and technology would homogenize the world. Yet today we confront new realities of pluralism at every turn. This chapter argues that we must be creative stewards of the new pluralisms we encounter.

1. If that which the church believes, teaches, and attempts to enact in life influences the world, then Christians must be ready to lead others into new patterns of life. In light of the pluralism of religions, how can we do this without arrogance?

2. We humans have a tendency to want others to conform to our patterns of being and believing. This is reflected in racism and imperialism of all sorts. How are these contrary to public theological principles that demand respect for democracy, freedom, and genuine pluralism?

3. Are there false forms of pluralism that can make idolatry common? Do you think that is found in "individualism"? In nationalism?

4. How is "pluralism within unity" an outgrowth of Trinitarian doctrine? Should all become Trinitarians?

5. Historically we have often been tempted to make Christianity an appendage of the family, the economy, government, or culture. What are the present dangers?

6. If the development of the modern professions is, at least in part, a logical outgrowth of "Christian vocation," what can we say about these professions?

7. Does the "professionalization" of modern society lead to "careerism"? Are the professionals you know more dedicated to career than to vocation?

8. If it is true that many modern institutions have been established by the teachings and actions of the churches in the past, what should the churches of today teach and do to reshape institutions in the future?

9. What can be done to better prepare Christians to minister in the world of today and tomorrow? How should theological education be expanded in seminaries, in colleges and professional schools, and in the churches?

10. In many ways it can be said that the modern church has become merely "empiricalist" in its understanding of reality. Do you think that we need a new willingness to look at life through the "abstractions" of theology?

11. Do you agree with Paul Tillich that we are at "the end of the Protestant era"?

12. Do you think it is possible to reconstruct a public theology of Word for the world of today? If so, what might you contribute to that reconstruction?

13. If the ideas outlined in this book become basic to a deeper and broader understanding of the nature and character of Christian stewardship, would you be inclined to increase your giving of time, talent, and tithe to the institutions that foster a public theology of this sort?